EAST ANGLIAN PRIVIES

EAST ANGLIAN PRIVIES

A NOSTALGIC TRIP DOWN THE GARDEN PATH

by

JEAN TURNER

COUNTRYSIDE BOOKS

NEWBURY · BERKSHIRE

First published 1995
© Jean Turner 1995
Reprinted 1996, 1998

COUNTRYSIDE BOOKS
3 Catherine Road
Newbury, Berkshire

ISBN 1 85306 344 4

Produced through MRM Associates Ltd., Reading
Typeset by Acorn Bookwork, Salisbury
Printed by Woolnough Bookbinding Ltd., Irthlingborough

CONTENTS

FOREWORD

This book started out as a fond personal memory of the outside privy. The joys and pitfalls of living with this mode of sanitation were very real to me. I lived with the outside loo till I was 24 years old. Father was a herdsman and so we spent much time in tied cottages and farmhouses. The outside 'bucket and chuck-it' was a part of our everyday life. Thankfully we always had large gardens. Perhaps I was too akin with nature but I never felt degraded or disgusted by this form of toilet. A little embarrassed at times perhaps when I reached my teens, especially when my 'civilized' boyfriends pulled my leg about our 'little inconvenience at the bottom of the garden'. Their cheekiness caused me no end of blushes. Whilst they basked in ease and comfort of inside flush toilets I merrily tripped my way down to the bottom of the garden when nature called. These were basics I had been used to living with and thought nothing about. In fact I secretly enjoyed the looks of horror on friends' and relations' faces when they came to stay. I never wasted much time in introducing them to our primitive privy. But then I always did have a suspect sense of humour.

I was acutely aware with some friends that my social standing could so easily plummet, but then I rather looked on our outside privy as a sort of museum piece. Something to show off and laugh about. By 1966, the year I reached the mature age of 24, everybody but us seemed to be flushing their cares away.

When eventually we moved to a large farmhouse near Beccles I was one of the first to glory in our flush toilet. At long last real soft toilet tissue found its way onto Mother's shopping list.

I have so enjoyed researching this subject. Everybody I spoke

A wooden privy in the woods on the Euston Hall estate, near Thetford.

to genuinely expressed an interest. The broad smiles needed no encouragement.

On a more serious note, the outside loo is fast becoming part of our social history. The amount of reading matter on this very important part of our domestic culture is scant.

I wish to thank readers of the *Eastern Daily Express* and *East Anglian Daily Times*, and the members of Suffolk East Federation of Women's Institutes, who readily responded to my letters inviting tales. Their letters enlightened and amused.

I would also like to thank the following for their assistance:

University of East Anglia

Norwich Central Library (Local History Dept.)

Suffolk County Council (Local Studies Dept.)

The National Trust, Blickling Hall

Last but not least I cannot and will not apologise for some of the words appearing in these pages. The word 'crude' may well spring to mind. The very subject attracts vulgar thoughts – without the occasional 'rude' word the very essence of this work would be lost.

So be warned this book contains some very down to earth research. The faint-hearted or fragile would be well advised not to even open it!

Jean Turner

[1]

HISTORICAL BACKGROUND

None of us stint ourselves when we visit our lovely, warm, indoor toilets. We stroll in, do what comes naturally, wipe our undercarriages on pretty, soft, toilet tissue and pull the chain – many times a day. We all take our modern sewage systems for granted and expect nothing less than efficient flushing wherever we go.

Yet it wasn't so long ago that our large towns and cities suffered appalling conditions which spread disease, and more than 50% of children died before reaching the age of five, that overcrowding was endemic and sanitary ware consisted of primitive pails, which overspilt into homes and streets. Overflowing privies and cesspools, coupled with poor drainage, allowed germs to breed, and pure water supplies were virtually non-existent or so far out of reach that the housewife had to cook in already polluted water. The resultant illnesses meant breadwinners lost precious working days. It is hard to believe but there were even some doctors in the mid-19th century who did not understand the connection between bad sewage and disease. The poorer classes living in urban areas had little choice or freedom; such simple rules as cleanliness were only a dream, and a trek to find water was often just too much of an effort after a long and arduous working day.

The aristocracy fared much better. They lived and dined in elegant homes, relying on wells, springs and rivers for their water. Their gracious establishments were generally built on high hilltops, and servants undertook the daily task of fetching and carrying water for domestic purposes.

It is interesting to note that water systems of sorts were repor-

Saved for posterity, if not for posteriors – an old privy used until two years ago and now under restoration by Clive Dunn of Norwich.

10

A medievel wooden closet seat found during excavations in King's Lynn. It is now housed at the town's Queen Street museum. (J. Arnold)

ted as early as 1169. The hall of the Palace of Westminster was supplied with water through lead conduits, although it wasn't until the mid 13th-century that these were extended into bathrooms for the king and queen.

Medieval houses of stature boasted privies. Sited beside a natural running water supply, privy towers were built, where lavatories were grouped together in a single structure, connected by shafts to the water or to sewage pits. Elizabethan and Jacobean houses relied almost entirely on close-stool – wooden seat contraptions, with a suitably-sized aperture and removable containers underneath. These close-stools were highly regarded and fitted out handsomely in rich materials which were, in turn, decorated with silk fringes. They were convenient, tidy and constantly emptied by household staff so as not to be offensive.

11

Many will be familiar with the modern day equivalent – the commode.

By the late-16th and early-17th century, indoor fountains, baths and water closets had been installed in some of the large country houses, the gentry proudly admiring each other's innovations. By the mid-18th century, however, water closets became less common, as a 'fashion' for outdoor closets had begun. In 1752, the owner of Felbrigg Hall in Norfolk, William Windham, began styling its 'little house', taking a great interest in the details of its design.

General lack of progress with sanitation was due not only to technical disadvantages but to lack of demand. Personal hygiene just did not rank very high in the 18th century.

By the latter part of the century, however, more efficient water closets had been invented although more often than not installations in houses were still supplemented by outside earth closets for the servants. Water towers were another invention. Serviced by rainwater, they proved quite ineffective at times owing to lack of precipitation. Lavatory cupboards were designed and a pinnacle of luxury afforded at long last, at least for the well-off.

Mr Edwin Chadwick and other reformers, against great government opposition, were responsible for the introduction of the first Public Health Act in 1848, which made it law for some type of sanitary arrangement to be made for every household. They felt impelled to act after visiting many of the poorer classes in their putrid smelling, overflowing homes, some containing sick people who could not get out of doors to dispose of their own excreta. Mr Chadwick and his followers often found it necessary to cover their noses with handkerchiefs and hang their heads out of the windows in an effort not to be sick. When one considers how far advanced the Romans were supposed to have been, having the capability of living in splendid sanitised luxury, with

George Manning of Spalding, using a traditional emptying scoop – the type once used by local councils on their weekly honeycart emptying sessions. Bearing in mind that many of the earth type pit toilets were only emptied once a year, it was little wonder that the operation took so long.

underfloor heating and water-supplied lavatories and baths, it is quite amazing to consider how governments allowed their population workforce to sink to such depths.

The second Public Health Act was introduced in 1875 by the Disraeli government. Vibrating with concern, politicians now insisted on every council appointing a medical officer of health. Later councils were encouraged to build sewers, street drainage, reservoirs, public parks and lavatories, libraries, wash-houses and swimming baths.

While city dwellers lived, up to then, with the stench of human waste, country people generally coped better. Rather like the animals they lived alongside, they used the open fields when nature called. In fact, until the latter part of the 19th century, most villagers just dug a hole in their garden and used it until full, when they covered it over with earth. It was only in areas of dense population, or where cottages were close together, without much garden space, that this method presented problems, as the accumulated sewage then tended to seep down the village streets or stand around in stagnant pools.

In the mid-19th century, earth closets made an appearance, offering not only a little convenience in the hygiene stakes but hospitality in the shape of shelter. Deep pits were dug and a construction built over them, complete with wooden seat. In the early days, this was often just a plain piece of plank with an aperture. Later, raised wooden seats were fabricated – a great improvement, as the squatting position required previously was not without accident. Human waste deposits dropped into the pit below, which was emptied once a year, with a long-handled ladle like a big soup spoon. Domestic refuse, such as vegetable peelings and ashes from the fire, were often thrown in as well, to reduce the scope of the odour. The annual 'shovel-out-of-waste' was conveyed to a specially dug-out hole in open fields or back gardens, providing excellent nutrients for the soil.

An early privy bucket.

Early this century, a much more efficient and hygienic method was introduced. The arrival of the bucket proved very popular although it was necessary to empty it once a week – or as often as it was filled. It certainly proved easier on the nose to live with. The pits were either concreted over or filled in with earth before the placing of the bucket underneath the holed seat. As one Suffolk man relates, 'At least when the buckets were installed, you didn't get the draughts that blew up from the pit below'. This bucket-type of outside privy container became locally known in Norfolk as 'bucket and chuck-it'. In Suffolk, they called it the 'bumby'.

[2]

DIFFERENT TYPES

Vic Haley of Poringland, near Norwich recalls:

'Around 1928, my father acquired a self-contained and semi-automatic toilet which was housed in an adjacent building. This was covered by a manufacturer's patent and from what I remember, it was an outstanding contraption. One got a feeling of insecurity when sitting down as the seat suddenly lowered itself an inch or so; when recovering the seat also recovered smartly and a quantity of ash was shot into the pail beneath. From memory this worked very well as long as the ash was well-sifted, otherwise a cinder put a stop to comfort.'

Although this may seem crude, the idea gives a fair reflection of the technical initiative that was available. Inventors were trying their utmost to perfect a system which offered a little sophistication when one wanted 'to go'.

The hopper-type loo, with its funnel-shaped container of soil or cold ashes, attached to the wall behind the seat, was definitely an improvement on what had gone before, and quite obliging in the case of smells. In Valerie Porter's excellent book entitled *Life Behind the Cottage Door*, she devotes a section to this subject.

The Reverend Moule's patented 'pull-up' earth closet (around 1860) threw one and a half pints of earth each time the closet was used.

Also in the mid-1800s, George Jennings, an important innovator of the Victorian era, invented a 'Servants and Cottage WC' with a varnished pine seat, which must have made the owners proud. As somebody pointed out, 'the earth closet may

16

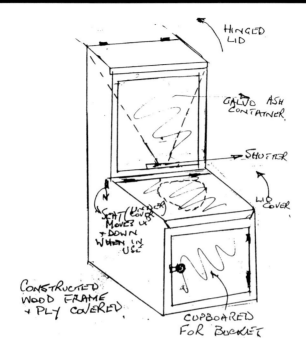

Labels within sketch: HINGED LID, GALVD ASH CONTAINER, SHUTTER, LID COVER, SEAT (LID COVER) MOVES UP + DOWN WHEN IN USE, CONSTRUCTED WOOD FRAME + PLY COVERED, CUPBOARED FOR BUCKET

A patented, self contained semi-automatic toilet, sketched from memory by Vic Haley.

pong a bit but it never freezes up'.

All sorts of variations on a good idea were developed, but the seating and hole aperture were fundamentally the same. With the hopper method, there was a small knob which the seated person pulled smartly upon completion of his performance. This knob operated a lever mechanism coupled to the hopper which in turn discharged some of its contents into the bucket below, covering everything up and leaving all neat and tidy for the next occupant. Of course it still had to be emptied when full but the whole was much more acceptable, especially to the ladies, whose sensibilities did not permit any mention of the lavatory at this time.

Mr Fred Mayzes of Blundeston has such a convenience attached to the end of a stable block at his listed Georgian property. It is believed to date from around 1840 or even earlier. Word has it that Charles Dickens came to the house at the time of writing *David Copperfield*. As Mr Mayzes remarked, 'It would be nice to think that my ancient loo had been graced by such a distinguished bottom sitting on it!'

It is worth mentioning here that the Victorians were wholeheartedly behind improvement in the sanitation stakes, and reform in this area flourished, at long last. The King's Lynn museum houses a collection of historical loos and chamber pots from this time. For example, there is on display a rather

Reverend Moule's patented design.

The 'Servants and Cottage' WC.

impressive early flush toilet, complete with blue flowers and leaf pattern inside the bowl. It is believed to have been made and installed by a Mr Johnson, who was, according to the King's Lynn directories, a registered plumber in the town from 1888 to 1904. Another grand looking specimen sports a lush pattern of pale blue wild flowers intermixed with oats and barley.

Perhaps the pride and joy of this unusual collection at King's Lynn museum is the complete Victorian closet manufactured by Shanks and Company, set in its own little room – a wash-down

A complete Victorian closet, manufactured by Shanks & Co, c1897. (J. Arnold)

version in white glazed earthenware, with a raised leaf decoration. It was removed from a house called the Gables, in South Wootton, near King's Lynn, where it had presumably resided since being installed in 1897.

We must remember it was not everybody who could afford one of the new patented models. For those living in the countryside, the introduction of the pail or bucket was sufficient improvement. Soon the 'privy' (defined in the *Oxford English Dictionary* as a 'private place of ease') became a permanent fixture in everybody's garden. The earliest and most basic construction consisted of corrugated sheeting covering the chosen site. This was perfectly adequate in fine weather, but come wind and storm it could easily blow over, sometimes with an engaged occupant inside.

Mr Bacon of Alby, near Norwich, recalls, 'I worked on a farm where we employed lots of ladies; they had several loos made from corrugated tin. As they moved so they shifted the loos to keep up with the job. One day a gale came up quick; some of them were being used and over they went. Legs and arms and other things were a sight to see.'

Of course, corrugated tin complains noisily if hit. Mrs Ann Kerr of Oulton, near Lowestoft, had trouble with brothers:

'Our outside loo was down the garden next to the coal shed. It was made of corrugated tin. We girls used to go in twos but sometimes we went alone. Often when sitting there 'doing our thing', one of the boys would chuck a stone at the loo. It was frightening – we were so scared that we didn't have time to pull up our knickers. We just ran hell for leather to get indoors.'

More rigid structures were gradually being built. Bricks and mortar were used for the walls and, what's more, brick floors and boltable doors came into vogue – the building of the privy had become a serious affair. This very necessary piece of architecture had, people realised, to be sturdy and well-ventilated. Often situated in exposed corners of a garden, it needed to withstand every kind of weather. Depending on affordability, outside privies came in all sorts of sizes. Whether it was a single-seater for a small cottage or a six-seater for a large family house, hard-wearing materials were of the utmost importance and lent themselves to individual design. The carpenter's job was crucially important – rough edges would not only have been dangerous but highly uncomfortable. For those of a meditating nature, bottom-branding would have proved too distracting.

Big ones, small ones, some as big as your head...

Mr Horsley, a retired builder from Bucklesham, in Suffolk, remembers when he was a rather green apprentice builder in Felixstowe during the 1920s. His firm had been asked to make a toilet seat for a four-holer; two seats for the adults, and two smaller, lower-down seats for the children. He asked how big he should make the holes. The foreman took off his bowler hat and laid it on the boards before drawing round the rim, saying 'the size of your head is the size of your bum'.

It must have been a rather hit and miss affair because folk are made up of all different shapes. For a petite lady to have to sit upon something designed for a pleasantly-rounded one is an intriguing thought. Somebody spoke of horrors worse than mere death!

Phil Colman of Old Catton recalls the time when he built a toilet for Roughton village hall. The blacksmith made the seat and cut out the hole. He said he got the size from 'Mrs ..., the fattest woman in the village'. Rough on the smaller females who had to keep their balance by pressing down on their palms; not easy when all hell is being let loose down below!

The biggest earth privy I have heard about was a six-seater, which must have been a pally sort of place, although I can't imagine a fair maiden wishing to sit beside her intended.

Four-seaters were popular too. Mrs Marcia Taylor remembers, 'My parents had a four-seater which was removed from their garden in 1973. It now 'sits' in the Ironbridge Gorge museum.'

Three-seaters and two-seaters obliged a large proportion of the country population. Ruby Ison recalls the family three-seater at the bottom of a very long garden at her childhood home in Northwold, Norfolk, in the 1930s:

'Ours was a three-seater, two for grown-ups and one, smaller, for a child. It was quite a performance when wanting to pay a visit in the dark. Armed with a candle I wouldn't go without our dog who frightened away the mice and rats.'

Two-seaters were very common and were favoured the most. A parent could sit comfortably beside their offspring and instruct in potty-training or educate about the outside world. The child would feel more confident – because children had been known to fold up like shut knives and disappear through the big holes into the murky depths below.

Mr E. Thorpe of Barking, Suffolk, remembers 'the small seat for little bums and the larger one for bigger. One day I decided that I could graduate to the larger and became trapped and had to be rescued.'

Not every child dreaded the visits, as Muriel Bird of Saham Toney in Norfolk recalls:

'My memory goes back 84 years. We lived at Hethel, near Norwich, amid woods and flower-filled meadows. We had a large garden and well away from the house, we had a coal shed, wash-house and the lavatory – a white-scrubbed wooden double, one for adults and one for children. Mother always used Jeyes powder and hot water to clean after emptying. During the 1912 floods, my father had to wade through deep water to carry us to the lavatory. He said it was almost a full-time job. It annoyed him how many times my sisters and I wanted 'to go'. We were enjoying the novelty.'

I will mention here that many refer to the outside privy as a lavatory when, in actual fact, the dictionary definition for that is 'room for washing hands and face, water-closet, urinal'. I can only think that some found the outside convenience so inconvenient that they were really wishing for something better when they referred to it as the lavatory.

My research has taken me all over East Anglia and, whilst the single-seaters proved quite easy to find, I experienced difficulty in locating a two-seater until I received a belated reply to my newspaper enquiries. It came from Mr and Mrs Bowles who live in a very large farmhouse at Scratby, near Great Yarmouth. Their letter was most encouraging. 'Here at Scratby, we have "a double" and "a single", they are not in particularly good order but you are very welcome to come and have a look.'

No sooner said than done. I arranged to go the first Friday in

A two-seater belonging to Mr and Mrs Bowles at Scratby, near Great Yarmouth.

A privy at Hempnall's Hall, near Stowmarket – a super 3-holer designed more than likely for mother, father and child.

March, which happened to be a day we had a fall of snow. It was bitterly cold but the sight of the double cheered me up immensely. Thought to be around 200 years old, it is a wonderful example, although not of the type where mother and child can sit side by side. It is an adult double. Looking in, to the left (not possible to see in the picture) there is an elegant little mantel suitable for a candle. The door disappeared years ago, giving the opportunity for a smart ivy to creep its way in. Sadly, the brickwork walls are deteriorating although anybody wishing to repair would have no trouble. The floor is charming, the same bricks used in the wall having been woven into a pattern. Torn up newspaper squares are still hanging by string from a beam above. It is a homely little place, just feet away from a side window in the farmhouse, and located in a pretty spot reached by a small private path. The single-seater belonging to this same property is around the corner and actually joins onto the double privy. When I was there, a bush of jasmine on the brink of flowering added the final splendid touch. I could have wandered about here all afternoon.

The majority of cottages had to make do with a single-seater, usually located down the garden path, in a straight line from the house. Accessibility was the keyword. Rushing out on a dark and frosty night in your pyjamas or nightie was fraught enough with difficulties. Finding the place had to be made easy. Mind you, there was no accounting for father's adventurous ways in the garden. A badly-managed manure heap, slap-bang in the middle of one's route, was one obstacle too many to contend with. Foliage looked interesting enough in the daytime, but come night time, it was a curse, especially if a sharp wind blew it across one's face.

These little outhouses were often built onto the side of sheds. Here are two examples for you to peruse:

I took this photograph on a very wintry, wet day – just to give you an idea of
how uncomfortable a winter visit might be.

Farmer, Mr Douglas Chubbock of Thurlton, outside one of his dignified privies. Unused since 1976, the interior seating has long since disappeared, making room for garden equipment. What endeared it to me was the size, barely room for a bum to position itself. Measuring just 32 inches wide and 66 inches long, with a height to the eaves of 70 inches, a person had to negotiate it very carefully. Douglas raised a laugh when he said, 'I should say there was only one way in, and that was backwards!' I especially liked the sensible placing of the fresh rainwater butt, plus the honeysuckle, which was creeping all over just waiting for summer. The birds too, were assured of a warmish spot (note the nesting box above the door).

Mr E. Thorpe of Barking, Suffolk, sent me this delightful picture of his grandparents' 'haunt'. It was only yards from the back door, and he remembers lots of ribald remarks – a cousin of his used to call 'Too late, too late, will be the cry'. What a pleasant, rural memory of a time when time stood still, apart from when you wanted 'to go' in a rush.

A poem accompanied this picture, entitled *The Little House at the Garden's End*:

'So distant from the cottage door (walls tarred a shining black)
Fall thirty steps or more, a tumbling annex to a shack,
On pantiled roof a house leek plant, a boarded vault with top all slant
Neath ivy laden bower, nestles the little slat-topped door.

A running figure leaves the house, in great urgency 'tis plain,
The Suffolk latch is quickly raised, the door slams shut again.
Minutes elapse at more leisurely pace, the figure moves, no more a race.

The Little House at the Garden's End.

I ask "Why hasteth thou, what sport?"
"No needless haste, I was took short!" '

Other privies were of the semi-detached or back-to-back variety. Quite embarrassing at times, as any sounds could be heard through the divide. As they were often shared between a number of houses, usage called for a degree of decorum. Pushing in when the neighbour was 'in situ' was a serious business, and taking friendship a bit too far.

This picture shows a pair of late-19th-century outside toilets. Entered through two plank doors, they were red brick, laid in

A pair of late 19th century privies at Oulton. Built of red brick, laid in Flemish bond, under a pantile roof which slopes down at the rear, they are entered through two plank doors. (Courtesy of National Trust)

Flemish bond, and the pantile roof sloped down at the rear. (*Courtesy of the National Trust*).

One Norfolk man recalls his semi-detached privy: 'I were sitting quiet as a mouse one morning, puffing on me pipe. I heard the neighbour go in next door. After a while, he shouted "How yew doin t'day Charlie?" I asked him how he knew it were me. He replied, "I recognise yar baccy smell." '

Country people were not all rough and unrefined – most observed the need for each other's privacy and went about their job in peace, although much amusement did take place.

Dick Mason of King's Lynn recalls: 'As a child in the Norfolk countryside, I lived in one of a pair of cottages, complete with bucket loo, well away from the house (desirable) and constructed of mainly local materials. Four wooden posts set in the ground, clad externally with feather-edged board which tapered side-to-side and overlapped in such a way as to be (at least nominally) weatherproof, whilst accommodating the very essential high level of ventilation. The roof was clad with good old Norfolk pantiles and therefore nicely weatherproof, at least in the vertical plane. Internal appointments were practical if not lavish; a wooden bench with two shaped apertures – one for each neighbour – below which resided a large bucket, the contents of which would be guaranteed to stifle the heartiest appetite even if only temporarily. It was the custom to smoke in residence – this has been scientifically shown to dull the sense of smell. Science, however, didn't figure at that time – just instinctive self-preservation. You will, no doubt, have deduced that it was perfectly feasible for the two neighbours to utilise the facilities simultaneously. A quiet wind – a boggling prospect which, however, did not happen very often, only during the visitations of what we would now call a tummy bug! Contemporary terminology was rather shorter and to the point!'

On the subject of colourful language, one delicate lady hated the outside privy and loathed even more the crude observations. 'At the risk of sounding dreadfully unsociable,' she explains, 'I must make comment on a dead or dying breed of countryman. When I lived in Norfolk, the price I had to pay for the privilege was the outside privy which was adjoined to the neighbours' – very decent hardworking farm labourers who left a lasting impression. I remember one going in straight after the other had left and the words "Yew datty buggar" are forever implanted in my memory.'

I personally remember my first introduction to the semi-detached privy at the end of the garden. I was just 13 and we had moved to Hales, near Loddon, to be nearer school. I liked the new situation but for the first time in my life I dreaded my visits to the outside privy.

I was of that age when boys had become something more than little squirts who tried to beat me climbing up the trees. Unfortunately, there was an extremely good looking young man about my age living next door and, worse, he was often to be seen marching to the little place down the garden path. In other words, his 'shituss' was attached to ours. Any detail in the form of shrubs or trees was sadly lacking, the semi-detached privies standing out like sore thumbs between the two gardens. I was so desperately frightened of meeting him halfway coming back from, or going down to, this shameful place, that I did despicable things in the chamber pot rather than go outside. I had to be responsible for subsequently discharging the pot's contents, but that was of secondary concern to me.

It wouldn't have been so bad if he had been gross and ugly, but he was quite the opposite – gorgeous, in fact. Life was rotten for a few weeks till I got to know him and regained my self-esteem. Although I steeled myself to rushing down the garden path, I was still on the lookout for him. I thought he would take a dim view of me doing the same as everybody else and my chance of friendship would be destroyed. But, of course, it was just silly me and my new hormones making themselves felt.

I remember the elements, too. The door of that same semi-detached hadn't seen much in the way of repairs, and it was a nuisance in the winter because we had to brush all the snow off the seat before sitting down. Cold comfort.

Mrs Smith of Hopton-on-Sea had similar troubles: 'We had an outside privy roof that leaked. We had to sit sometimes with an umbrella up. Ah, but country people were hardy.'

It seems natural to presume that the vast majority of privies were sited at the bottom of the garden for a reason. Thankfully, during the heat of summer, the smells were not absorbed inside the house. Another advantage was that the long trek back was often utilised to good effect. Householders might snatch the opportunity to gather asparagus, celery and any other vegetables from the garden, for the kitchen. However, a number of farm cottages were well-endowed with buildings only feet away from the back door – a wash-house, with a copper for boiling on washday, a coal shed and last, but not least, the privy.

[3]

PRIVY DESIGN

This messing about outside wasn't all doom and gloom. On the contrary, most people knew nothing else. I did once hear of somebody naming their outside privy 'Misery Palace', but others called theirs grander names such as 'the Houses of Parliament'. Mr Bacon of Alby mentions, 'Hanging up behind our privy door was a little ditty in the form of a soft wooden scroll. It went like this:

"In Houses of Parliment where notes are made,
The first thing a member does is uncover his head.
This little place is the reverse,
The first thing a member does is uncover his..." '

Once the privy was built, individual households took great care in design – that's very pretty, pity about the pong.

The majority of doors opened inwards. It left little space for manoeuvre, but then a person wasn't going there to dance. It made for privacy. On a fine day, if the coast was clear, an occupant could sit and enjoy the beautiful countryside. Mrs Joan Alden of Surlingham reflects on her recollections of the outside privy: ... 'some with almost affection, others with utter horror, especially as a small child on a long trek at night with only a candle in a jam-jar for illumination; a rustling in the grass from a mouse or rabbit, coupled with the swinging shadows cast by a fragile light in a trembling hand, brought all sorts of unknown terrors. Yet in daylight these places were nothing more than a grey wooden shed or outhouse at the end of the garden, but they did have a character all of their

A single-seater, still in excellent condition although it hasn't been used for 'for donkey's years'. Note how the door opens inwards. Notice also the magnificently placed ventilation point at the top. Raised high enough not to have any nuisance value, it was created by leaving out three bricks.

The inside of this cute little building has not been cleaned out for years – the reason for all the straw. See the small cavity on the right – there is also one on the left behind the door – little spaces for lamps or candles in jam-jars. No bolts on this door.

own. One we had was a bonus – it had a hole in the door through which, if I bent down a little, I could view limited parts of the garden. I could watch chickens scratching in their run, see the dog in his kennel, but best of all I could see if anybody was approaching which was important because we shared this toilet with the next door neighbours. There were seven of them and so there was a continual flow of people much of the time.'

Sightseeing was all very well but there were times when the door which opened inwards (a feature of all the outside privies I have come across) came into its own – it was possible to kick it shut with a foot.

Air vents were an obvious necessity and came in all sorts of guises. Some were just high-up holes, whilst others were attractively patterned iron plates built into the wall. Artistically designed doors with ventilating patterns were another fashionable feature which allowed in some light, not bold enough for prying eyes but large enough to see the stars and let out steam. To be sure, one didn't need to be a detective to know who had gone before. Most had their very own personalised leaving smells!

It must be said that most doors were just straightforward affairs. Nothing particularly smart, merely functional.

John Powling of Downham Market was not so fortunate, even comparatively recently. He writes, 'My wife and I married in 1954 and used an outdoor bucket loo with a sack nailed over the exit to keep out the wind. We were there for two and a half years.'

Loraine Stedman of Little Stonham, in Suffolk, took this picture of her dilapidated outside loo. Originally a two-seater, all inside evidence has practically fallen away over the years. The inside is now well overgrown. The door is a lovely sky blue, the walls cerise. Last used in the early 1950s, it is surprising how well the paint has stood the test of time. This door had an iron latch which merely hung down when not in use – pushed around 270° clockwise, it slotted into an iron holder. It did have a lock. The outside has, surprise, surprise, a window. Very unusual. Lorraine thinks it probably had glass in at one time. All in all, an ivy-clad piece of local history. This privy is situated 30 to 40 yards from the house, down a narrow path, and built over a narrow ditch at the north end of the house. It was constructed of Suffolk brick and was beside an old clay lump wall, 12 inches thick. In recent years the pantile roof collapsed, followed by the back and one side wall. The ivy is holding it all together now.

Although some privies did cater for modesty, with bolts on the

The Little Stonham loo door.

inside, most were just fitted with a simple device to keep the door shut. The frail and elderly were vulnerable and locks would have caused much bother, particularly in the case of older people who might be tired out after their lengthy trek down the garden. The only security was usually a latch or a very ordinary DIY hook and eye feature made out of steel wire. These were not fitted tightly, springing and jumping about in windy weather, and so could quite easily have been cut from outside with a pair of pliers.

Locks on privy doors were rare. Shouts were very common.

Mrs Joyce Preston of Gillingham, near Beccles, recalls, 'We didn't have a bolt on our door and if we heard someone coming, we would either start coughing loudly or singing.'

Mrs Kitson, who lives near Ipswich, remembers their outside door proving something of a nuisance in times of gales and high winds (meteorologically speaking):

'When blowing a gale outside, we would be sitting there going about our business and the door would fly open. We could not shut ours properly and the first instinct was to jump up and close it. This was not always possible so we had to just sit there and hope no one would see us!'

She also adds: 'I often think how easy my children and grand-children have things nowadays but they will never have the memories that I have of my childhood.'

Yes, try as we might, it's difficult to forget the well-trodden garden path.

In my time, I have found many privies with notices inside. I can't remember where I saw it, but one displayed a baffling sign, 'Please do not touch exhibits' (as if!).

My own dear mother tried to preserve some dignity; this photo-graph was taken in 1952, when I was ten years old. Father was a cowman and, at the time, we lived in a three-bedroomed semi-detached cottage at Caister St Edmunds, near Norwich. The notice on our outside privy door is difficult to read but, in white paint, it said 'Put lid on please'. Pity mother did not also add 'Please close door after use'. We were such an energetic lot I doubt we would have found time.

The picture shows my mother's sister, Aunt Dolly, pushing my two younger sisters in a wheelbarrow. Jennifer is on the left, and Shirley, aged about two, on the right, looking none too excited about her ride. I am the tall girl standing at the rear right and next to me is our neighbour's daughter, Christine.

My own family privy in 1952.

Lids were a MUST, always neatly made to fit into the bum-hole aperture. Most sported a sweet little knob for easy removal.

The Lid
Whether you are a grown-up or a tot,
If you don't replace, you are a clot.
Insects bite!

Wintertime was bad enough, but summertime minus a lid just didn't bear thinking about. Flooring was normally concrete. Here again, the housewife created some degree of interest with linoleum covering – this very practical material served the family well. Mats and carpets took a lot of maintaining since the outside situation encouraged much in the way of muck and mud. Autumn leaves, too, blew in without a by your leave. It must be said that some privies were reduced to the absolute minimum in the furnishing stakes but there were those house-proud women who took as much pleasure in the appearance of the outside privy as they did in their house.

Mrs S. Leathers of Thurton, near Norwich, fondly remembers her aunt and uncle's outside convenience:

'We had to walk all round the outside of their large old farm-house to reach it. Inside it had two lovely wooden seats, one for adults and one for the children. This fascinated me as we only had one. On the floor, Aunt had a nice rug and on one side was one of the old-fashioned washstands complete with bowls and jugs of water and soap in a dish, and a towel to dry your hands. There were books to read to pass away the time and these were kept neatly on the washstand. If it was dark, there was an oil lamp to light and candles and matches. The light in it at night made it even more attractive to me. All in all, I thought this was a very superior lavatory on a grand scale compared to the one we had at home at the George and Dragon pub.'

So there was a certain amount of etiquette and charm surrounding the outside privy and, although I am glad we do not have to use them now, I feel we have lost something precious in the countryside – even if it is only natural manure for the gardens and a chance to get some fresh air into our lungs late at night. Indoor WCs have made us lazy and dimmed our exploration of nature's beauty.

I, personally, cannot remember any interior decoration that went on, as far as wallpapering goes. Indeed, some did not even get as far as plastering; most that I remember were just plain brickwork. However, many housewives did cover this true state of affairs. Most just lightened by whitewashing annually,

The snug entrance to a one-time four-seater can be found in the kitchen garden wall at Castell Farm, Raveningham. It was quite a hidey-hole delight, surrounded in summer by jasmine and in winter by the winter-flowering variety. All four positions were serviced by one deep pit at the rear. No evidence remains of the inside.

although some went to town with pastel colours. Perhaps it was something to do with circumstances, because John Linder of Banningham recalls, 'As a lad, I lived in a row of four superior cottages; the loos were situated about thirty yards away, in a row of four. These were superior in that they were painted and wallpapered inside.'

Outside features were quite luxurious. Gardens were big business years ago – the man of the house growing all vegetable requirements. His keen interest extended to the privy, turning an uninviting place into something attractive with flowering creepers, rambling roses, bushes and trees. Pam Rowe of Saxmundham remembers the horse-chestnut tree that stood outside her privy, 'My husband reminded me of how he once stood waiting for me with a hurricane lantern. The wind was blowing and the conkers were falling on top of his head.'

There are always jokes associated with the outside loo – but it is sometimes difficult to know whether they have in fact been made up since. Knowing the East Anglians as I do, I put my money on this retort being given at the time. Country people were never short on repartee, always giving as good as they got. The story goes:

One visiting townie remarked after a visit to 'that funny little place down the garden', 'My word, you are trusting – do you know there is no lock on your er ... toilet door?' To which the down-to-earth owner replied, 'No, and we've nivver had a pail pinched yet!'

[4]

WHAT NO PAPER?

As teenagers and having discovered boys, my sisters and I went to great lengths with our limited knowledge of dress sense. Matching white gloves and shoes adorned our flowery outfits in summer. Nobody, least of all us, gave any thought to our bums, which, underneath it all, must have been tinged black with newsprint.

The world of toiletries is big business today. It is possible to purchase toilet paper in colours to match the bathroom, soft, shiny, recycled, quilted even. All commercial treats for the backside. In outside privy days there were no fussy, inherited habits where wiping the bum was concerned. In the very early days before the invention of nice, brick-built privies, folk bopped down in any old field or space and used whatever was at hand, literally. Leaves and grass tackled the problem, although it goes without saying that nettles were avoided. After a shower of rain, a handful of wet grass did a magnificent job in cleaning a dirty backside. I know. Born and bred in the Norfolk countryside, many is the time I have wanted 'to go' whilst out playing away from home. There was nothing to it and all perfectly natural as far as we country kids were concerned. Otherwise, for centuries people used old rags and washed them – it wasn't everybody who could read or afford a newspaper.

By the turn of the century, however, newspapers were considered a daily purchase-must. Remember there was no television and radios were only for the better off. The daily read was recycled and used in the outside privy. Some 90% of the population wiped their backsides in this way. Comics and magazines, too, adapted well, although it must be said that the shiny sur-

Outside toilet with lean-to roof, 1864. Red brick laid in a mixture of bonds –
stretcher bond to east flank, Flemish bond to south side. (Courtesy of National
Trust)

faces of magazines were more hindrance than help! A few
households luxuriated with 'Izal' and 'Bronco' toilet paper,
which again rather slid across the surface. Children were often
given the job of cutting up the newspapers into suitably sized
squares and pronging them onto a holder, a nail proving an
extremely efficient tool.

Apparently, many a child learnt to read in the outside privy.
Mrs Joyce Preston of Bungay recalls, 'I do remember the paper
used to be newspaper but sometimes we had old comics. It was
most unfortunate if the piece you wanted to read had been used
by someone previously.'

Mr Thorpe of Barking, however, preferred the *News of the
World*, 'it was softer and provided a bit of spicy reading.'

Double outside toilet, north-east of the outbuilding. Early 20th-century. Red brick laid in a stretcher bond under a sloping roof clad with corrugated asbestos. Two plank doors with catches and hinges. (Courtesy of National Trust)

Mrs Dunn of King's Lynn always knew where her father was going because 'Dad always took his own paper. He would crumple up the paper in his hand after placing his cap on his head.' Her father was no fool. 'I remember getting to the privy sometimes after a particularly damp patch of weather only to find the newspaper all cold and soggy. Not very nice at all.'

Some had to wrestle with pets, as Phil Colman of Old Catton recalls, 'The seat in our lav had two holes, one we used and the other had a wooden box over it which mother filled with newspaper. In the spring, mother's hens laid their eggs in the box and it was quite a job trying to get a piece of newspaper without being pecked.' His mother must have stuck up for her broody birds because Phil Colman goes on, 'Broody hens would sit on turkey eggs later in the year. We were not allowed to disturb the sitting hen until she had hatched out the eggs.'

Of course, if a family had to share a convenience, jealousy could rear its ugly head, as Dick Mason tells us, 'Sacrosanct to each neighbour was the supply of toilet paper. No, not on a roll, silly – torn up newspaper on a nail. My first introduction to the *Eastern Daily Press* – but I mostly preferred the *Beano* which I confess was only to be found on next door's nail.'

Country wives were nothing if not practically minded, full of common sense, and very much aware of extravagance. That is why they kept the lovely soft tissue-type paper that oranges came wrapped in. A real treat, which was saved and offered as an indulgence to special guests.

Could you use hymn sheets for this purpose? No, neither could I, but an old story goes like this...

A young married couple had viewed a house near Lowestoft, with the intention of buying. On returning home they suddenly remembered they had not seen or noticed any toilets. They wrote to the vicar who had shown them around and asked where the WC was. Imagine the couple's surprise when they received the following reply...

I regret to say the WC is six miles away which is rather unfortunate if one is in the habit of going regularly. However, it may interest you to know that many take their lunches and make a day of it. Some can spare time to walk, others go by train to get there in time. I personally have never been and the last time my wife went was twelve years ago and she had to stand the whole time. By the way, it has been made to accommodate about 1,000 people and it has been decided to replace the wooden seats with plush velvet ones to ensure comfort for those who have to sit for the full proceedings. The Minister stands in full view of everyone so it's not difficult to hear him as he is a bit long winded. I can assure you the WC is a very popular place and those who go leave something behind and come away feeling much relieved. There are special facilities decided over by the Minister who gives help if needed.

Yours sincerely

the Vicar

P.S. The hymn sheets behind the door are for your personal use.

The reverend gentleman, we are to suppose, was ignorant of the term 'WC' and thought they were referring to the Wesleyan Chapel.

[5]

RATS, CREEPY CRAWLIES AND OTHER VISITORS

Of course, the outside earth closet is now regarded as something amusing. Mention it, and ears prick up as the grins widen. We British just adore toilet jokes. But it wasn't all fun when a person encountered a fly blown privy. A hazard not only to one's health but to one's anatomy.

Blood poisoning was a reality in summertime – and screams were the order of the day where we females were concerned. Outside earth closets were a magnet to insects, a real treasure trove of pure filth. Rich pickings indeed for a variety of creatures. However meticulous the housewife in scrubbing the seat, however dutiful the man of the house in disinfecting the new pail, assorted wildlife came rushing in, by every method of propulsion, including wings and – the extreme of creepy crawly horror – eight legs. It was sheer hell. Imagine, if you can, a couple of bluebottles buzzing around underneath when you wanted to sit urgently upon their only available means of escape.

As Mrs Peggy Knock of Mendlesham, in Suffolk, points out, 'The cobweb in the corner suspended between the whitewashed ceiling and wall, minus the spider, had us all wondering – where is it?'

All sorts of things hovered below, just waiting for a lovely, white, plump backside! It was a very brave person who sat straight and went red in the face with strain whilst keeping a beady eye out for long-legged creatures. The anxiety was fuelled by reality, although imagination played a big part. If you could see the creepy you were left worrying in case it fell off its perch. What if it went down your back or, worse, between your exposed thighs? What if one of the in-flight insects happened to be of the striped variety with a sting in its tail?

Mrs J. Kitson of Ipswich was brought up by her grandparents at Rendham. They had an outside 'bumby', and in summer the flies were a real problem: 'Grandma had a sticky fly-paper hanging up – my grandparents often got their hair caught up in these things and yet the blue bottles never got caught. They seemed to be aware of the sticky paper and were always buzzing around in the most unlikely of places.'

I, personally, didn't mind the daddy long-legs type of spider. They were much more sociable and slow, hanging around the backs of doors and on the edge of the air vents. I have a great love for them and I think it's entirely due to sitting and watching them whilst 'on the throne'. These were certainly places from which to observe nature.

Mr Burlingham of Dersingham had a pair of swallows that nested and bred their young each year over the loo door: 'Each year too, some sort of fly used to lay its eggs in the droppings beneath because when I was a young lad, being nosy, I looked through the hole in the seat and it used to be literally heaving with maggots.' Lovely!

One countryman who lived near Norwich in the late 1940s found his outside toilet a marvellous hiding place for stashing away his gee-gee winnings. He hid his monies behind the 'in-use' bucket under the seat. 'All sorts of things were thrashing about below there,' he recalls, 'It was as safe as the Bank of England.'

Rats, too, found the warm smells inviting. They were a nasty menace at nights. They hate being cornered and so it was necessary to kick the wooden seat to get them out before plonking yourself down. Some people took their pet dogs and sent them in first to sniff around and frighten away the vermin.

Children loved playing tricks on their friends and found enormous enjoyment at night. Pat West of Leiston was no exception, remembering, 'I often watched moles digging under the nearby bush and practised yodelling to our pet duck, Charlotte. I used to frighten my friends with creepy shadows when we went there at night with the bicycle torch.'

Talking about bicycles, Jean George of Marsham had an outside privy at the end of a 60 yard long garden – 'Whenever I wanted to go, I simply used to get on my bike. It was quicker than walking.'

However one travelled to the outside loo, the trip 'home' was as a general rule more leisurely. Even in your own surroundings, this journey was not always straightforward, as Carl Adams of Loddon reflects, 'As a youngster living in a house with no modern conveniences, the old brick lavatory was about 40 yards down the back garden. Many a time my mother lighted a candle which blew out on the journey down, plunging me into pitch black; I would often smack into mother's linen prop.' Certainly, soldiers must have been made of the same kind of stuff as us!

Earlier this century tramps were a part of the landscape. They walked the roads, quite innocently, cadging food and drink from

Survivor from a bygone age!

anybody who would entertain them, more than happy if some-body would oblige and fill their billy-cans with tea. Many offered them bread and cheese out of pity. But these fellows were quite crafty, so it seems. Not content with the hedgerows and woods, they longed for something better at times. Taking risks passed away the time, no doubt.

Mrs J. Porter of Harleston, in Norfolk, remembers her mother talking about intruders: 'As this was a rural area, the only facility was the bucket and chuck-it at the bottom of a long garden. One morning before school, she was ordered to use the toilet. On arrival, she found the door locked. Grandmother was sum-moned: she waited – eventually an unknown person came out, jumped over the fence. Naturally he was watched. He found their loo very comfortable and used it regularly. Later a plan was hatched to put an end to this intrusion. A couple of days later, my uncles and mother hid in the surrounding bushes observing this man entering their loo. They waited until they heard a rustle of paper, lifted the back flap and stuck a very large bunch of stinging nettles up against the intruder's rear parts. As you would guess, the man never used their loo again.'

Mrs Mary Phillips of Wereham also had trouble with uninvited guests: 'Before the Second World War, when I was a child, we lived in a cottage, one of several clustered around a yard. At the bottom of the yard were the closets. The nearby main road was much frequented by tramps as it led to the nearest workhouse. My mother was always of the opinion that our lavatory was being visited by them as it was of the pail variety and would fill up very quickly.'

[6]

AND STILL IN USE...

As we anchor ourselves on our inside flush toilet, spare a thought for those who still use an outside privy, by choice, for those who seize the opportunity for some fresh air when they need relief.

It may seem rather unnecessary in this day and age but it isn't everybody who favours indoor warmth. One old couple recently offered modernisation shrank from the very idea. The proposal was to convert a pantry near their back door, but they considered the whole idea distasteful and quite unhygienic. No

One of the bachelor gentleman's downstairs sitting rooms. Nothing has changed for decades. In fact, his mother decorated this room when in her late 70s (over 40 years ago) and the wallpaper is still as good as when it was hung.

A view of the outside buildings. The privy door can be seen on the extreme left, the middle door opens into a still complete wash-house, and the third door into a shed.

way were they going to use such a place within spitting distance of their kitchen sink. Dreadful! Awful! Should never be allowed!

Another old gentleman, who was converted, had this to say about his new, inside comfort-station, 'At least when I used the outside privy, I had something to show for all the grunting, straining and farting. Now it's all mysteriously flushed away!'

Most of those still using an outside earth closet are getting on in years. On the whole, they are surprisingly happy and healthy, putting down their advanced age to plenty of hard work, exercise, fresh air and home-grown vegetables.

There is a certain bachelor gentleman living in Suffolk, who is 90 years old, and continues to use an outside loo. He also bathes in a tin bath once a week. His home is rather like turning back the clock 90 years – nothing has changed since his

A view of this bachelor's 'modernised' privy. He did let me down on one score – he now uses 'real' toilet paper.

mother died a few years ago at the grand age of 107. She also used the outside privy which is approached by a brick pathway just yards from the back door of their farmhouse, until a week before she passed away. His outside facility was originally of the pit type, emptied annually, but this gentleman 'modernised' his privy over 40 years ago. He took out the wooden bench seat, filled in the pit, and bricked a square surround which covers the pail. The top, which now boasts a 'proper' toilet seat, opens to release the bucket. 'A local man was paid to carry out the annual emptying task but the stench during transit to a bordering field became too much and so that is why we converted it,' he explained.

His brother and sister-in-law live close by in a bungalow. This brother also refuses to use an inside flush toilet if at all possible. In fact, on a rare holiday (his first in 41 years) to visit relatives in Canada a few years ago, he demanded they brought their outside privy back to life, for his private use. As he says, 'A rat never makes a mess in its own house!'

Mr G. Thurlow, who lives near Ipswich, also owns up to still using a pail toilet. 'I have never lived in a house with a flush toilet but as I am 73, it doesn't seem to hurt me but it's still embarrassing when people come round.'

I shouldn't worry, Mr Thurlow, after reading this book they will probably envy you your outhouse.

Mrs Swain of Felixstowe writes: 'I was born in a little village in Suffolk where my parents both lived until my father died at the age of 94, my mother having died earlier. Their outside loo down the garden path about 30 yards from the cottage, was hidden in a belt of trees until they were blown down in the 1987 gales. This loo is still being used today by my two bachelor

This housed the couple's two-seater and was used till about 1988, by which time the knots had fallen out of the wood and winter nights had their 'chill factor'. A wren built a nest inside every year. This dear little privy was nicknamed 'Camouflaged Karzy' by their son-in-law.

59

A new site was chosen for its replacement, pictured here, and rather than hide it the owner did a good paint job to last him and his wife well into the 21st century. As it looks rather like a grand sentry box, one would not be surprised to see a guard with a gun, standing outside, on duty.

This one belongs to the National Trust and is notable in that the privy is still in use today. Truly 'as pretty as a picture', it is an early 20th-century example – red brick in stretcher bond, under a sloping roof clad in corrugated asbestos sheets. The plank door has a catch and strap hinge.

61

A lady who wishes to remain anonymous sent me this interesting picture. As you can see, a modern privy on the right provides for any visitors although it still has to be emptied. 'Some cheeky lads painted the sign on the seat for a joke. I remember once being very frightened when I was on the loo in the pitch dark. The door was open wide when something jumped onto my lap. It was the cat.'

brothers, both in their 70s. I suppose people often talk about these places and remember them, but not many use them these days because of hygiene and, of course, they are out of date.'

Mrs Carol Carpenter from Hardley, in Norfolk, has no complaints, 'Yes, I have an outside loo. Admittedly, it is the flush variety and not a bucket type, but my husband, myself, and two small children, have lived here for the past thirteen years and are very happy living with it.'

Mr Chatten of Ilketshall St Lawrence, near Beccles, remembers getting quite a shock when he was doing some building work for an elderly lady just a few years ago:

'Whilst working, I was bursting to go to the toilet and so asked the good lady if I could use her loo. She said "Yes, but it's an outside one." Off I went – I didn't mind in my condition. Upon entry I noticed that instead of the big pail, there was a gallon jug and it was full to the brim. I scampered to the nearest ditch!'

Mrs A. Flegg of Ipswich still feasts her eyes on the bucket loo but, thankfully, she says, does not use it any more. 'We have been here 35 years and were using the outside bucket loo up till about four years ago. We had the pantry made into a flush toilet. It's great now that it's indoors.'

Now, in case any of you think this sort of thing only happens in the deep, deep, countryside, spare a thought for some who live within 45 minutes of London. Mrs Sylvia Moss of Aldeburgh, in Suffolk, had a cousin living in Chelmsford, Essex, barely 30 miles from London, who was using the outside type until she moved eight years ago.

These are only a handful of examples, but statistics point out that possibly 1% of the East Anglian population, at least, are still living with, and using, the outside earth bucket.

[7]

'VERY STRANGE', SAID THE TOWNIES

The story goes that a very important city feller, affiliated to a sports club, came down to Suffolk one weekend to enjoy his favourite sport. Much beer swilling, eating and merry-making went on after the game. Staying with a country member, he was roused in the early hours with an upset stomach.

'Where is the toilet?' he asked, after rushing around the house like a mad thing. 'If you only want to piddle, thar's a buckit thar', his host pointed towards his night-time, indoor convenience. 'I feel sick', said the important city feller. 'Then yar'll hatta go down tha gardin', the host returned, unrolling his own furred tongue.

All haste and minutes later, the important city feller churned out the contents of his stomach. Unfortunately, his false teeth refused to stay put and landed in the suspect pail beneath, amongst the unmentionables. In panic he called for his country-man host, who, much divorced from the seriousness of the situation, laughed like the proverbial drain, fumbled about down below, and retrieved the important city dweller's teeth.

Once back in town, he told his story, 'My god, I'll never forget the incident. Jimmy washed them under the tap. Putting them back was pretty difficult, I can tell you.'

City relatives and friends always associated the outside privy with squalor. The countryside was a dirty enough place, especially around the farms, so the earth closet just added to their worries and confirmed their worse fears – country people were a lot of rough diamonds, characterwise. How could we possibly accept and live with such crude sanitation? Going down the

This pretty outside privy belongs to Rona and Nobby Lear of Blaxhall, in Suffolk. Untouched by person or time, it has been lovingly preserved. Flanked by tall lilac trees, this 200 year old brick building is almost covered in ivy.

garden to spend a penny was not much better than sipping tea out of cracked china. Needless to say, the townies partook of, and thoroughly congratulated, the vegetable garden. Sharp-brained they were not!

Socially, the outside loo was a bit of a come-down. City folk found there was little grace attached to plonking their bottom over a pail full of other people's waste. No doubt this lack of appreciation for the facilities kept them amused over dinner parties back home.

Trouble was, city cousins loved to visit in summer when the gardens were at their best. The ever-present danger of wasps and flies caused much commotion when they tripped down the garden path for relief. But, as one favourite uncle joked, 'Nivver mind abou' em me beauty, fart and you'll gas the buggers out.'

Townies, we found, could never quite understand, or accept, the natural cycle of waste. The tomatoes, for instance, that they enjoyed on the tea plate, germinated themselves easily. They passed through sweet lips into the stomach, out into the earth closet, were buried in the back garden and grew without attention.

Visitors often had to be quite courageous when it came to beverages. Too many cups of tea meant frequent visits down the garden path. Plying guests, who absolutely loathed the outside convenience, with lots of refreshments, was a mean trick but it happened often enough.

Mrs Sylvia Moss, of Aldeburgh, remembers the 'bumby', 'I was staying with family in the country, years ago, and I heard the honeycart come round in the early hours of the morning to empty the outside privy. One of the men remarked about the very full pail, "Company – I should think they have had company!"'

Of course, many relationships blossomed between townies and country folk. Setting aside the inconvenience, the countryside was an appealing place to live. When a young lady from town fell in love with a country boy, she had to learn to forget about flushing and remember to keep an eye on the outside privy pail. It was an amusing adjustment.

One such lass who survived was Mrs Joan Garwood of Barton Mills: 'I married an agricultural worker in 1940, and as a townie used to all mod cons, the bucket up the garden came as rather a shock but I coped. Incidentally, we always had the most wonderful vegetable crop – I wonder why?'

During the Second World War, many youngsters were evacuated to country areas. Imagine how they must have felt after leaving their parents and being confronted with a back garden to 'poo' in. Mr Thorpe of Barking remembers two who found it all too much: 'During the early part of the Second World War, two boys were evacuated to us from Ilford, Essex. After a few weeks, their parents visited and I shall never forget their looks of horror after visiting our 'toilet'. Not long after this happening the boys went back home to face the blitz rather than rural sanitation.'

Another true tale, where evacuees preferred facing Hitler, is recalled by Mrs Ruby Ison. 'We had some evacuees during the war – they had never seen anything like it. They didn't stay long, which wasn't really surprising.'

A spinster lady living in the heart of Suffolk laughs about one incident: 'We had an evacuee, a lovely child who soon settled into our family way of life, including our excuse for a lavatory outside. Her mother came to visit on one occasion, obviously pleased to see her child so well. After her visit to the privy, she came back into the house and said, "Cor blimey, the scent of unknown flowers!" '

Former members of the Home Guard are always full of stories, and recollections of outside sanitation are among them. Mr C. Brown of Fairstead, near King's Lynn, writes: 'An octogenarian, I was a member of the Home Guard during the Second World War. One night during the invasion scare, we were on duty on the outskirts of King's Lynn. At about midnight, some distance down the road, appeared a swinging dimly-lit lantern, accompanied by clanking of heavy iron wheels. This caused some speculation by the guard. One local man came out with the remark, "It's the Iron Duke". The arrival proved to be a horse-drawn container on iron wheels – its purpose being to empty the sanitary pails in the area. I can assure you this caused a good deal of amusement and comment by the personnel.'

[8]

THE HONEYCART

Who, in their right mind, would want a job on the honeycart? What a thing to have to put on your CV. But somebody had to do it and, after all, it was job. What's more, it wasn't connected to market forces, so the job was secure.

As somebody pointed out, 'What do kings, poets and beggars have in common?'

Whilst most country households had the unenviable task of emptying their own privies, towns were serviced weekly by the council. A vehicle, aptly named 'the honeycart', went round regularly, usually at night, disposing of the smelly stuff. Some called this conveyance 'the Iron Duke', as it was merely a tank on wheels drawn by two horses until motorised power came onto the scene. (Many Norfolk people, from more than one area, remember the horses were named Bugger and Sod no doubt due to expletives.) Of course, the posher-type people called the thing the 'night soil collection vehicle'; other descriptions included 'the violet wagon', 'the lavender cart' and 'the perfumed garden'. Did somebody mention 'humdinger'? Australians, too, relied on such a service, and called theirs 'the dunny cart'. Indeed, it was difficult not to make bad jokes about it in whichever country you lived.

Here again, in summertime, the stench was a little off-putting and households tended to keep their windows shut on emptying night. During winter, the contents of the honeycart, if leaked onto a road, made for an unusual skating rink. The workmen must have hated the cold weather – the combination of frozen hands and the smells moved them at a terrific pace.

There was no strict timetable attached to the expedition, and

Rona and Nobby Lear's restored emptying shute.

often a person was sitting when the collectors called, 'Sit yew still my bewty an finish. Iyll cum back inner minnit.'

In Keith Skipper's book, *A Load of Old Squit*, he does not overlook this part of social history. He mentions Litcham's legendary Wally Feeke and his honeycart escapades.

A certain Mabel Riches allowed Keith to tell her tale. Apparently, one evening she was sitting peacefully outside when all of a sudden 'Bang! Crash! Screech! Rattle! The bludder thing's nearly full!' Wally was at it again. Mabel shot up, screaming, into the air. She ran back inside in a highly distressed state, her knickers round her ankles. There was a trapdoor at the back and the luckless Wally had emptied the pail while Mabel was still busy above.

The interior of the Lear's remarkable restoration job, showing the stunning condition.

Wally used to own a meadow up the Tittleshall road from Litcham, and on this blessed plot he emptied the contents of his cart in a man-made pit. In winter, this would freeze over and form a perfect skating and sliding rink. Norman Wagg and his mates found this to be an ideal spot for getting rid of all their youthful energy. One day, they were going full pelt, probably practising for the Winter Olympics. Suddenly, poor Norman made a cracking exit with a considerable splash. There he was, chest high in it. Despite the high sides, Norman managed to clamber out, emerging like a dripping, smelling creature from another planet – 'I got a master's ding of the lug and a good thwacking as well when I got home.'

71

Ex-policeman John Mutimer of Kimberley, in Norfolk, remembers when he was stationed at Aylsham:
'Up to the early 1940s, most of the houses, shops and other premises, had bucket toilets and this included the police station. The 'night-cart' man had a full-time job. In my time at Aylsham, the man in control, if my memory serves me correctly, was called Jimmy. A short, stocky man, with a heavy apron or wearing a filthy old gingerish coloured coat. He used to hang this coat over the shafts or on the small platform where the shafts joined the body of the cart. One day this coat was handed in at the police station as lost property. We didn't need to trace the owner! I returned it to him but the smell hung about the station for days after. I am now 73 and until a few years ago, the night soil lorry used to call at some cottages nearby; they have since been modernised.'

Accidents will happen. Roy Chamberlain of Hoveton said his father often told the following story during after dinner speeches, always maintaining it was true:

'George, Fred, horse, and honeycart were on their round one summer's night. The cart was nearly full and, being rather warm, George took off his jacket and laid it on the side of the honeycart. Unfortunately, one cart wheel dropped with a bump into a pothole, causing the jacket to fall in and sink slowly. George considered the situation for some minutes, then rolled up his sleeve and proceeded to grope around in the tank in an effort to get it out. Fred came back to enquire what was going on and when told, expressed the view that really the jacket would not be of much more use, "Um not worrid abou' t' jacket", George replied, "Um tryin' to get me sandwiches out o' the pocket!"' '

[9]

NATURAL MANURE FOR GARDENS...

Whoever said recycling and organic vegetable growing was new? We had it all in days of yore with the outside loo.

The laws of nature prevailed – there was a sense and structure to the world of nature when the majority of country people lived their lives close to the soil. Life was a natural merry-go-round! Recycled human waste acted as a high-nutrient manure, frightening off pests and resulting in bumper crops, and organic vegetables were a feature of our mealtimes. Adjacent trees produced huge amounts of excellent fruit, for, as one lady said, 'What came out of bums was good for plums.'

Before the arrival of the bucket, the pit-type outside privy which was emptied annually, could take anything up to three hours to be cleared and its contents buried in a marked location, either in a nearby field or in the garden. The marking was very necessary because a person would have quickly ended his or her life if they had fallen in. Wind directions were taken into account prior to the emptying, and it was carried out after dark when all women and children were shut up safely inside the house, with the windows and doors closed. A large ladle on the end of a very long pole extracted the human dung into a sizeable wheelbarrow. Husbands were extremely vigilant on these occasions as a temperamental barrow in charge of this waste was an impediment they could do without. Sons of the correct age assisted – under careful guidance. Other methods of disposal included scattering the waste over the entire garden and digging it in the next day. Mixed with straw, it did the soil a world of good.

The later, and more well-liked, pail was emptied much more

frequently, perhaps once a week, depending on usage, thereby avoiding the sickly smells associated with the long-term pit closets. This also allowed for a fairer distribution around the vegetable garden. As one man sensibly explained, 'When you dug up a root of spuds, you emptied the pail into the hole.' Access was gained either by lifting the whole top seat and pulling out the full pail, pulling down the front and extracting the same, or via a rear door, outside – an extremely dodgy entry, which could wreck friendships. Once open, the back entry exposed a substantial part of one's anatomy, and boys being boys ...

Needless to say, the weekly burying session was solely a male task. A widow woman could always call upon a good, reliable neighbour to bury her waste. The pail was flushed out afterwards with disinfectant, sometimes lined with newspaper, before being returned to its rightful place.

Alan Page of Stowmarket sent in the following true tale: 'Between the years 1926 and 1940, there lived opposite us an elderly Victorian spinster lady, the daughter of a former vicar. She was kindly, generous and quite stout; her bottom protruding in mallard-like manner. She had a small income and by arrangement, she used to take in the illegitimate children of the better-off until they could be placed. She also offered holidays to some of London's slum children. This old lady was known as 'the nurse' or 'Nurse Doughty' and she named her house 'The Nest'. In those days, every house had a good, old, bucket lavatory except the rectory where, I am told, the pong and odours were confined indoors. My late father used to be prevailed upon by the nurse to empty the lavatory for her. And so, one summer's evening, after having been hard at work all day and after that, working on his allotment (and keen for his pint at the pub), he asked my mother what time the old lady got to bed. He was told that it was usually before 9 pm. So, at 9.15 pm, he duly set out with his spade to set about the task. Now the lavatory had a fixed seat, access to the bucket being obtained by the lifting of a flap from behind, much in the same way that the flap on a man's jacket can be lifted. My father lifted the flap and pulled out the pail when from within he heard knockings and great commotion, followed by a loud squeal – the nurse had stayed up later than expected!'

On the subject of the unexpected, Mrs M. Dunn from King's Lynn remembers an occasion when one of her brothers, who was a coal delivery man, 'opened a door and nearly tipped the sack of coal out onto an old lady's lap. She calmly said, "Next door, please, in the shed." ' Mrs Dunn also goes on to say, 'We had to work hard as Mum had ten of us but everything was always spotlessly clean. Mum disinfected everything with boiling water from the copper. On moonlit nights, my dad and the neighbour would lift their buckets and proceed to take them up the back garden to a small orchard where the fruit trees got well-manured.'

And so, emptying was but a natural cycle in a very natural world. Those of us who lived with the outdoor earth closet were quite probably immune to germs. All the many people I spoke to about the outside situation, voiced the same opinion, 'the vegetables were wonderful and picked only hours before serving. We very rarely heard anything about heart attacks.' But then, exercise and fresh vegetables were the order of our days. Besides which, life was less stressful. Very few had to go far to their workplace and, if they did travel any distance, it was by bike.

Not only did the vegetables take root in ideal conditions, nettles thrived too. The nitrogen from years of manure enrichment secured healthy growth. In fact, this enrichment came

The 'gardner's entrance' to an old earth closet in Belle Vue Park, Lowestoft.
(J. Arnold)

from livestock sources as well as human because many country people kept the odd pig for the table. These animals were fed on leftovers and boiled potato peelings (Ah, I remember the lovely, earthy smells of potato peelings being boiled!). Free-range chickens too, scratched their way around the garden, and hunting for the chicken-fruit was a fun pastime for the children – the rewards of finding a full nest of eggs underneath some obscure piece of garden machinery in a far-flung corner of the garden made for a happy ending.

Many of the younger generation wonder how we managed to survive, let alone live, alongside such primitive sanitary conditions and, what's more, talk about it eagerly and fondly. Of course, we knew nothing else. Certainly, we ate the vegetables which grew willingly in the waste, and we suffered no lasting harm. It is only because we now have such super-hygienic comparisons that we begin to question.

Although I have fond memories of the subject of this book, they are probably all bound up with my happy childhood. I began my research full of nostalgia but, having come across the 'real thing' again, I thank the Lord for the creation of indoor sanitation. Why, the indoor bathroom or WC is good enough to take lunch in!

Mrs Beulah Howing of Ludham recalls the time when her parents were publicans of the Kings Arms, in the village: 'The lavatories were primitive and smelly. Large galvanised buckets caught the waste. Carbolic powder was used lavishly. Situated in the backyard of the pub was a separate and a double, facing each other which caused much hilarity among the Grouts factory girls from Great Yarmouth on their annual outing. Their squeals of excited laughter finding that we lived in the Dark Ages and the loan of the scullery to repair their make-up in the mirror above the stone sink (no hot water) was watched in awe by me. The artistry of vivid lips and darkening of lashes and much fluffing of permed hairdos.

We also had a pit lavatory in the 1930s in the stable yard. The usual wooden seat but with a brick arch, with the residue being racked out into a triangular pit which was surrounded by a brick wall. This wall was an ideal height for a see-saw. My friends would be persuaded to mount the plank on the smelly side. Was it accidental or intentional that I occasionally fell off leaving them to fall into the quagmire and squelch?' It seems that some children had very narrow escapes.

Phil Colman of Old Catton was a crafty youngster: 'I always kept my collection of birds' eggs in a box in the corner of the loo. I thought it was the only place a policeman or game keeper would not look. The emptying of the pail was a secretive thing. Father paid his cowman, Frank, sixpence a week to empty ours in the garden. The plum trees in the middle of this patch always had a record crop.'

[10]

PERSONAL TALES FROM EAST ANGLIA

Before starting my research, I placed letters to the editor in the *East Anglian Daily Times* and the *Eastern Daily Press*. I received an enormous mailbag of personal experiences and anecdotes which have proved an invaluable source of information. If I had any doubts about whether there would be enough to record, these were quickly quashed. All those who wrote did so with great fondness of heart – and, as well as a unique insight into how previous generations lived (and please remember it was not that long ago), a very warm atmosphere of family togetherness shone through the pages. I will not 'mess' about any more but peacefully sit back and let others educate and inform you.

David Henshall from Stutton was an evacuee, from the London of 1939, who finally ended up living with his paternal grandparents in Pulham Market, Norfolk. He was at one time Executive Editor of the *Evening Standard*, later Deputy Editor of the *Evening News*, more recently Editor of the *Ipswich Evening Star*, and currently, in retirement, a columnist for the *East Anglian Daily Times*. He writes:

'In 1939, I remember many of the Pulham Market homes were still lit by oil lamps and probably only the squire, the doctor, and perhaps a handful of others had indoor flush lavatories. My grandparents, Edward and Edith Henshall, kept the Falcon, a nice old pub which faced the equally attractive Crown Inn, on the other side of the green. Just in front of the Falcon was the tall pump, with its long, weighted handle which supplied the village with water. The Falcon had a two-holer with buckets underneath which were used by both family and customers. They were emptied, along with those of the rest of the village, once a week by a man with an "iron constitution", into a horse-drawn tanker, known as the night cart. However, this was wartime, and once quiet village pubs frequented by a few card, darts and domino playing locals were shortly to become heaving, noisy centres of care-drowning jollification packed with men from RAF Pulham, local army units and several American air-fields. Their cups did runneth over and so did the buckets! Behind the outhouses at the Falcon at the outbreak of war was my grandfather's pride and joy – his bowls green, flat as a bil-liard table. It broke his heart but he allowed it to be turned over as part of the "Dig for Victory" campaign. The turf was sold to the vicar, the Rev Stacey.

'It was here the "bumby" overflow went and the size of the cabbages, carrots and beans grown in this patch were a constant source of wonder to everybody except me (then about 12 years old) who, for extra pocket money, undertook the dread dead-of-night task of emptying. As a consequence, I went right off home-grown vegetables for a very, very long time. My mother Rose later fled the London Blitz and supervised a bomb-making factory in one of the remaining huge hangars at RAF Pulham. Not generally of a nervous disposition, she refused to go to the Falcon's privy at night unless accompanied by someone; this invariably turned out to be my grandfather who, wind, rain or snow, would stand guard at a discreet distance outside.

'The waste incidentally, was also used to fill pits and big holes on local farms. Covered with soil and ash, in time it turned into excellent land.

'A school chum and I had one of these sites pointed out to us by a farmer's son, but my foolish chum, a townie like me, refused to believe what was under the hard crust of ash and jumped in. He disappeared up to his chest in "sweet violets".

'It is not without interest that my sister Madge, who became a GI bride in 1944, marrying into an Ohio fruit farming family, discovered that rural America was just as lavatorially backward. Her first home there had a privy at the end of the garden, the only difference was that it had a friendly snake curled up on a shelf near the roof.'

C. A. Vanston from Gillingham, Norfolk, remembers: 'I lived with my parents and brother in a town where our loo was at the bottom of the garden although it was a flush. All my school holidays were spent with relatives in the country where the loo was halfway down the garden in a shed over a pit and the bench seat was a double; one for an adult and one for a child, to sit side by side. I used to have nightmares that I might fall through. I married during the war and our first home was a cottage (all we could get) in the country and, again, our loo was at the top of the garden. The large bucket was emptied weekly by the honeycart. We didn't endure this situation long because we found enough space in one of the bedrooms to make a little room (more of a cupboard) but large enough to accommodate a flush toilet. When, after four years, we managed to find a modern house with a bathroom and all mod cons we thought we were in seventh heaven. My children and grandchildren eye me with disbelief when I relate these tales.'

Mrs Thrower of Bunwell, writes about a farm remembered from her childhood: 'Just before last Christmas, on a sunny, spring-like day, I had reason to call at a farm I used to visit as a young girl some 40 to 50 years ago. You can imagine my anticipation. The farmer was friendly; farmhouse, gardens and lawns immaculate. Walking around the fields, I could see for miles but all the old hedges, shrubbery, orchard, meadows and pond had gone. No sign of any bird or wildlife at all. On the way home, I

A view from the bottom of the garden path. A brick-built privy with a pantiled roof at Silvergate. (Courtesy of National Trust)

could not help but remember the way it used to be – busy, busy farm workers around, tending cart horses, cows and calves, pigs in their sty, chickens and geese that used to frighten the life out of me when I had to visit the 'thunder box' at the end of the garden. The hand-pump in the yard, no electricity, piped water or central heating, tin baths on Friday nights. If I could choose, would you wonder which part of the clock I would change?'

Muriel Fall of Bures, Suffolk, can now look back in amusement: 'Way back in 1947, I was staying with my husband's mother and father. The privy was down the garden, inside a shed. During the night, I had terrible stomach pains so I had to trip outside to the privy. It was locked and I couldn't find the keys. My husband came down thinking he knew where the key was. I couldn't wait any longer and had to bob down in the garden. I don't think the shed was locked any more after this!

'There were seven in my own family and we had to almost queue but it was the duty of everyone to put a shovelful of ashes in the pail before we vacated. I once followed one of my brothers: he had put hot ashes on and my goodness, the hot air rose to my bottom – a thing I've never forgotten.'

Peggy Youell is a member of Ipswich Morning WI. She formerly lived in Darsham. She remembers plenty: 'Oh yes, I remember. There was the wash-house where the clothes were boiled in a copper, heated by a fire underneath and then put through the wooden-rollered mangle. Behind that the two loos, back-to-back, to serve two houses.

'When I was small, we spent quite a lot of time with my grandparents since Grandad was ill and my dad worked away quite often. Their loo had a small one at the side 'just for me', I was told. I guess it helped with my potty training. Obviously I thought I was special. As time passed, my parents bought the house next door and after Grandad died, I slept at grandmother's as she didn't like being alone in the house at night. One night, in my early teens, I awoke with strong stomach pains – an urgent call to that place at the bottom of the garden. Not stopping for a light, I dashed out into the dark night and alas, halfway down the garden I fainted – how long I was out cold I don't know, but imagine the state I was in when I came round to find an apparition in a white nightgown hovering over me, and me in a real old mess! My dear grandmother had heard me go downstairs and thinking I was rather a long time had come to find me, armed with the night light she always burned. A wash in cold water soon brought me back to reality – no hot water on tap and it would take too long to heat anyway.

'My husband tells me he remembers that where he went to school, there was a door at the back of the loos which dropped down for access to empty, and that naughty boys would wait until someone was sitting comfortably and then open the door and pop in a bunch of stinging nettles or the like. What a way to pay back a grudge!'

Greta Towler, Narborough: 'Did you know that the scoop on a long handle which was used for emptying the pit was called a 'jet'? Many years back, Grandad used to laugh about a mate who smoked a pipe of tobacco. This friend had a pipe, with a large bowl. Grandad used to say it was "like an ole jet".'

Mrs Janet Crissell of Bacton WI recalls: 'My husband and I remember the outside privies very well. I remember using one when I was ten years old – it always had lovely leaves trailing nearly all over it which turned to lovely, different reds. We always decorated our baskets of fruit and vegetables with them for the harvest festival. We would often visit my grandmother: her privy door didn't fit very well and we would watch the neighbours go by to do their gardening. A friend of mine said they lived in a block of cottages and had to share their privy with the neighbours who often made them wait (how awful!). My husband said they always had to rattle the privy door so that the mice ran out before they went in. They also had a neighbour who always sang *Fight the good fight* and *O God our help in ages past* in his privy.'

Mr Richard Weeks of Brisley writes: 'This might be of interest to those who served in the Western Desert – we used a 3 ft × 3 ft × 3 ft box (approximately) with the bottom knocked out and a hole cut in the top. This seat could be slung somewhere on most armoured or other warlike vehicles. You never knew how long you were going to halt anywhere but it was the work of only a few minutes with an ordnance engineer's shovel to exca-

An overgrown privy at Holt Road, Felbrigg. (Courtesy of National Trust)

vate a small trench, pop the box on top of it and there you had a "thunder-box". It's interesting that the word "loo" (from the French "lieu") should have come back fairly recently. In Shakespeare's time, "jakes" was the usual word (French "jacques") and the Americans still retain "john". The cry of "gardy loo" will be familiar to many as people emptied the contents of their chamber pots from upper windows into the street.

'In a mansion in Northamptonshire, I have seen a dining room that had a permanent vomitorium (marble) at one end, and have heard that in early Georgian times, a commode was usually provided for the use of gentlemen after the ladies had retired. Whether it was screened or not I don't know but doubt it. My great uncle, who was a fine gardener in Tunbridge Wells, supplied his guests with the usual washbasin and jug, with hot water brought in a copper vessel swathed in a towel. The residues, including the contents of the ubiquitous chamber pots, were all tipped into slop pails by the maids and then taken down to my uncle's library. The contents were applied to his roses; the soapy water killed the aphids and the rest nourished his plants.

'I am an avid reader about the navy in Nelson's time. In warships then, the "heads" were just below the bowsprit and, consequently, regularly washed by the sea. Officers had their own arrangements in the stern. However, in John Company's ships, full of young ladies on the way to India to find husbands, the "heads" were replaced by the "roundhouse" which preserved some elements of modesty. Somebody once wrote in one of them:

This bloody roundhouse is no use at all
The seat is too high and the hole is too small.

'Beneath which, another wrote:

Your comment provokes the obvious retort –
Your arse is too big and your legs are too short.'

Mrs Janet Chambers, Eye: 'At the tender age of three, I had just learned "to go" by myself, but being a small child had great difficulty in climbing onto the wooden seat. Once this was achieved, it required a rather tricky balancing act over the wide aperture. Still, confident I could manage without calling mother, I reached for the paper and this was my downfall; I needed both hands to grip the seat and once I had leaned sideways, with one hand raised, I slipped, unable to prevent myself from sinking into the ghastly, stinking, morass below.

'A more recent memory concerns the early days of marriage. Although we had the benefit of a form of flush, with rather hit and miss home plumbing, it was still situated some distance from the house, in a dark, cobweb-filled building, next to the cow shed. Some relatives from London arrived for the weekend, accepting our quaint country ways with fortitude. Cousin Lil, dressed most unsuitably in a tight skirt and high heels, answered the call of nature one morning and returned to the house ashen-faced and screaming that she had been attacked by a wild creature. Our fierce bantam cockerel who was as good as a guard dog, had taken a fancy to Lil's nylon-clad legs. The cousins departed soon after this incident, never to return to Suffolk.'

Mr Alfred B. of Smallburgh: 'Years ago, in a neighbouring village, there used to be Dilham Broad. It was used to service a lock on the now defunct Dilham-North Walsham canal. No longer used, the broad drained away and is now grazing land for cattle. On coming to Smallburgh, I met an elderly, retired, farm worker who was brought up in a cottage near Dilham road. A dyke trickled its way across the bottom of his garden and the "loo" was built over the top of it. His father claimed it was the first closet built in Norfolk with running water!'

Mr S. P. Cornish of Buxhall: 'Every school holiday, I was sent to relatives who lived on a farm in Horringer. I loved every minute and the only loo we had until 1956, when mains water was laid on, was up the garden. The original pit under the wooden seat was filled in after one of mother's cats fell in and thereafter, an enamelled pail stood under the hole. Mother used to spray the little house with Flit, in a spray gun, daily to eliminate the flies; the whole interior was whitewashed and smelt of Jeyes fluid, which wasn't unpleasant. It couldn't have been too bad because we used to take our comics to read in there and at night, a Tilley lamp to light the way; then we didn't stay too long because the shadows scared us to death. My biggest spanking was caused by the little house, or rather the need to use it. Once we had been put to bed, we were supposed to stay there. However, feeling in need, I led the three of us up the garden. To do this without being noticed, we got out of the bathroom window (the bathroom had a bath with a pump to the copper in the kitchen below but no loo), down the dairy roof and jumped off onto the grass beneath which was a matter of five ft. Unknown to us, Grandma was sitting in the kitchen, with the dairy door open to get a cool draught and saw three little phantoms flash past the fly screen on the dairy window – giving her one of her "turns". Grandad shot outside and caught us creeping back and I got a hiding for frightening Gran, as I was the ringleader – happy days – oh I forget, there was a sprawling honeysuckle which almost covered the privy and we usually left the door open so we could see to read.'

Laurie Payne, Bury St Edmunds: 'A story – a retired colonel and his wife, both of whom were of considerable proportions, were viewing a country cottage, one of a row of three, as a possible retirement haven. They found the cottage charming and just what they were looking for. Asking about the toilet facilities, they were conducted to the end of the garden to a row of three very narrow wooden huts. "Ere ye be sure", said Josh, "orl in fust clars order." Glancing at Josh's broad shoulders and those of his wife, the Colonel remarked, "This is ridiculous, we could not possibly tolerate such a place, why there's not even room to turn round, however do you manage my good man?" "Well sur", said Josh, "in the country yew av tew git used tew a lot o' different ways, an oi've niver ad any trouble yew see, oi allus unarness outside an' thin backs up and in." '

From a lady wishing to remain anonymous: 'Forget bonnets and Easter bunnies, bee stings are not nice. In fact some people are allergic to them and have to be taken to hospital. You can imagine, then, what the reaction would be if one got in your knickers! When I was a small girl, like everybody else around us, we had a shed in the garden with a bucket loo. Ours had some sort of flowering plant around the outside. I was always on the go, playing outside, and after a rushed, very necessary, trip to the outside shed, I bopped down near the door to wipe myself clean. The shrub was busy with bees and Mother always warned us to keep the door shut but ... fear the worst, because it happened to me. Somehow, I must have trapped a bee between my dress and knickers because when I pulled up the latter, I was stung in a very private place. There was no lasting harm but I did have to lay embarrassingly at full stretch on the kitchen table whilst mother and a neighbour (called by Mother, in panic) searched me out.'

Harold Leeder is in his 90s and an ex-Waveney resident. He was employed in the building trade years ago and found the outside privy an excellent place to plan or solve problems. 'Whenever I was missing, the other lads would laugh and say, "Harold is in the loo sorting out the next job." '

Dick Mason, King's Lynn: 'As a child, I loved to tinker with mechanical things, as I still do, but most of all I was fascinated by explosives. Materials for such projects were scarce but carbide was available – more correctly carbide of calcium. In appearance, this was rather like small, greyish pebbles which, when moistened, gave off acetylene gas, which is highly inflammable and can also be explosive if ignited in a confined space. This I knew, from earlier experiments, and from there it was a very short step to my privy bomb. Wishing to include a shrapnel feature, I decided on a strong, glass, screw top bottle as the basis for my bomb, knowing that a little carbide mixed with some water inside would produce gas in abundance. All that remained was to ignite this and – BANG! For this, I would need a fuse. As always, like a good countryman, I utilised available materials – binder twine. This is a coarse string used to tie sheaves of corn and available in abundance at the time. I would soak some in paraffin (used for household lighting) and it would surely burn. It did. All experiments finished and the day of the great explosion dawned. I rose early – but where to carry out the test firing to good effect? Ah, the loo! So I placed my bomb on the seat, led my fuse under the door, pinched my mother's matches and lit the end. The other end went into the bottle via a small hole in the screw top. I retired behind the shed and waited, and waited. Please God, let me have my explosion. My prayers were instantly answered and my explosion went beyond my wildest dreams – it was ear-shattering. And, of course, also loo shattering as well. Feather-edged boards fluttered about like autumn leaves and when the dust settled, I beheld a scene of devastation of blitz-like proportions – at least as far as our toilet was concerned. The four corner posts held fast, as did the sturdy roof tiles – the seat was still there in all its glory, somewhat blackened, but intact – but all vestiges of privy privacy had gone. Mum and Dad were understandably displeased, totally unable to appreciate that they had bred a potential atom splitter. Our garden rang to the sound of hammer on nail as Dad made good the damage, whilst I made myself scarce. Mum and the neighbours did their best to contain themselves!'

Phil Colman of Old Catton: 'Memories of Hill Farm, Rougham, 1926-1930 – my brother George, sister Beryl and myself lived at Hill Farm, and in the winter, after tea, Mother would order us all to go to the lavatory which was 100 yards from the house. As I was the eldest, I had the candle, Beryl held the back of my jacket, and George was trailing, holding the back of her dress. We would slowly make our way up the path in between four large yew trees, in which perched 40 turkeys and 20 hens, all making weird noises. It was quite scary. When the wind blew out the candle, Beryl would scream until I got it alight again. When we got to the lav, Beryl would go in with the candle, shutting the door, leaving us out in the dark. George, four years younger than me, would shake with fright, and Beryl would keep calling out to me to keep talking so she knew I was still there. When Beryl came out, George went in. When he came out, I took them back indoors and went back on my own which took all my nerve.

'Then, when I was 14 years old, my father and the schoolmaster, Mr E. Coe, started a village hall committee. The toilet, at that time, was made of corrugated iron, one side had a drain for the men, and the other side a loo for the ladies. This rather basic arrangement was not popular with the ladies. A committee meeting was called, an estimate secured. My father jumped up and said, "My son will make one for half the price." I made the toilet and went home feeling very proud because a little card sat inside, stating "Made by P. L. Colman". The next dance at the village hall went well until 11.30 pm. Somebody came in the hall to say somebody had turned the new ladies toilet on its side. The smell and mess were terrible. The committee paid £1 to a Mr Matthews to clean it up. Next day, I fastened it down with stakes.'

Mrs Joan Alden, Surlingham: 'In the several moves we have had in Norfolk, we became the owners of some quite attractive toilets, in that they were screened from view by climbing roses and periwinkles wherein the occasional chaffinch would nest and so provide a seasonal point of interest. But the best one we ever had was when, in 1964, we found an old, unmodernised cottage and brought our children to enjoy the delights of pastoral basics. Up until then, from my childhood, it was the duty of the man of the house to weekly dig a hole somewhere and, towards evening, open the little door at the back of the lavatory, withdraw the bucket and empty it forthwith into the prepared hole.

'Now here we were, in this ramshackle little cottage with no running water but a soft water tank and a well, a nice stretch of garden, with a bucket loo at the end of it, and furthermore, progress was far enough advanced to have someone else come and empty the bucket. The council provided the "night soil man" who came every Friday night ... A minute's hesitation and the cry would go up, to the horror and shame of the occupant, "Hang on, Harry, thar's an ol' hin on the nest!" This toilet faced the wall of a neighbour's cart shed, which on our side was covered in japonica, honeysuckle, and forsythia. What a pleasure it was to sit with the door open, in contemplation of the beauty of the flowers and the complexity of a man walking on the

A large brick-built privy at Hall Farm near Metton. Note the two small bucket shutes. (Courtesy of National Trust)

moon. Nobody knew you were there, not even the people waiting opposite for the bus. Somebody in the family suggested there was a certain devilish satisfaction in the knowledge that one can do one's own thing in front of a crowd and not be seen.

'On the day we moved to the cottage, I suppose it was inevitable the children would soon want to use this "abominable" excuse for a loo. Having previously been weaned on proper toilet rolls, none of which could be found at that precise moment, they were suddenly aware of how primitive we had become when I handed them a sheet of newspaper, with the explanation "That's all we had to use in my young days." Having later located a toilet roll, I took it down to "the shack" and there on the back of the door was a portion of the said newspaper stuck there with the one word "PHEW" in high, capital, letters. I found this so amusing that I began to hunt through the remaining paper to find something equally appropriate, and came up with "THERE ARE HARD TIMES AHEAD". Someone found a delightful little scenario from a magazine, "She: 'WE MUST GET OUT OF THIS STINKING HOLE, JACK.' He: 'YES DARLING, WE'LL MOVE AS SOON AS THE NOISE DIES DOWN.'"

'Over the years that we lived there, numerous friends and other members of the family contributed to the decor of "the shack", and when finally we left, it was covered from top to bottom, side to side, with an early vogue of graffiti. Everyone came away from the place with a happy smile and chuckle or two. We now live in a modern house, with bathroom and toilet in a pristine condition, all clinically white tiled, running water, and a flush to take away impurities. But to this day, we talk with almost an affection and certainly with a sense of adventure, about our outside loo. It just needs someone to say, "Do you remember...?"'

Mr C. Bacon of Alby, Norfolk: 'In the late 1940s, a young lady, with a son, lived down a lane past us. Her husband was in the Navy. Her house stood in a meadow surrounded by cattle in summer. In winter, they were shut in a yard not far from her house. To get to her loo, she had to go out of her garden, across a bridge and over a ditch near the bullocks. She had no pail but a big hole bricked up under the loo with pipes coming in from the bullock yard was a type of "drainage system". The farmer stacked little square bales of straw along the outside wall and this is where the story begins...

'The muck in the cattle yards got higher and higher, with the littering, till it managed to reach the bales. One windy day, the young woman went to her loo, leaving her little son indoors. I guess the bullocks pulled out a bale and let the whole end of the stack fall down, completely covering the door of her loo. She was there all night until the farm workers came to feed the next morning. She says she passed out three times during that time. By the way, my uncle was a gamekeeper. In his loo, he had a reserve paper box and reared lots of game with the help of several bantams in that box.'

Mrs Ella Piper, Diss: 'I well remember dark, wintry nights, when my three sisters and I would decide to go. Mother would light a candle for us and off we would go, hands around the candle in case it blew out. We would go purposely to laugh and talk together. We enjoyed that time on our own and did not notice any smells.'

Mrs B. Dent, Cromer: 'I had a very strict father and I was only allowed out socially once a week. During my early teens, I would arrange to meet my boyfriend at the garden gate at 9 pm. The gate was at the bottom of a long garden, near the outside privy. At 8.55 pm, I would fetch a torch and candle, which I left in the toilet. I then had a kiss and cuddle for 20 minutes. It has always puzzled me why I was never caught. Did Mother suspect, I wonder? I could have had serious bouts of diarrhoea!'

Mrs Joan Garwood, Barton Mills: 'We always had friends and relatives staying with us during the summer months – embarrassing moments would crop up when I had to take my husband to one side and hint that the bucket loo needed emptying. We tried to carry out the rules of hygiene as much as possible, by having a box of sawdust to hand to cover the contents and also a very large container of Jeyes powder – a pinkish powder with a strong odour. When my husband had been laid up in the past, I had to do the emptying operation myself – no joke with snow on the ground and hard frost, but we got by.'

Mr John W. Mutimer of Kimberley: 'As a boy, I lived with my parents in Suffolk. Two of my father's sisters were married to farmers in the Debenham area (Church Farm, Framsden and Moat Farm, Framsden). I often used to visit and stay with them on occasions, more particularly Church Farm as there was a cousin of my own age and, being a boy, he and I got up to all sorts of tricks. Both farms had the so-called "earth closets". I remember the one at Church Farm very well. It was close to the house, with a garden and pond at the back, with an elder tree close by. I suppose there is some reason for it but to my knowledge all earth closets seemed to have an elder tree nearby. My cousin and I used to carry out pranks on visitors using this closet, such as going round the back and opening and slamming the lid on the emptying chamber.

'Upon joining the Norfolk Constabulary, my first station was at Aylsham. I was in lodgings at 19 Sir William Lane, with a Mr and Mrs Daniels. This house was semi-detached, built in the 1930s. We had a bathroom and flush toilet, as did our neighbours, the only ones in the area. Drainage was into a cesspool not a septic tank, and, in the main, this was used by visitors. We used the bucket toilet at the bottom of the small garden. There was no mains water and we had to hand-pump the water from a well in the neighbour's garden. I used to take my turn at pumping – turn the lever to our house, then pump away, filling the tank in the loft. We used to groan a bit when visitors used this loo as this meant extra pumping.

'In March 1951, I was transferred to Haddiscoe as a uniform beat officer, living in the, then, police house on the hill next to Arthur and Phyllis Wood. We had a bucket toilet, they had the luxury of an Elsan, but of course, we both had to bury the contents in the garden. At this time, my two daughters attended Toft Monks School, with its own primitive outside toilets. All the farm cottages in that area had bucket toilets and nobody thought much about them at that time.'

Mrs A. Cain, Fakenham: 'I was a cleaner at West Raynham village school for 38 years. Until flush toilets were put in, a man emptied the school's four buckets every weekend. I knew by the smell on a Monday morning that he had emptied onto the school gardens. Not a nice job, scrubbing the seats on a Friday, with the buckets full!'

Mrs Mary K. Phillips, Wymondham: 'In the 1940s, I was employed as a maid at an inn in west Norfolk. In the yard of this hostelry, adjoining the stable-cum-coalhouse, stood a small, unlit, wooden-floored closet, containing a two-holed wooden seat. It was of the earth type, not bucket variety. Two loose wooden boards covered the holes and it was my duty to scrub them every Friday night. The boards were scrubbed each side and stood up to dry. The run-of-the-mill lady customer would be directed to this convenience. There was an upstairs WC but, at that time, every drop of water which entered the cistern had to be hand pumped up from the kitchen so it was not in common use. One evening, I was serving in the bar when a woman customer went to the outside loo. I do not remember if she had a torch but, anyway, she said she sat down over one hole and put her handbag by her side. She had a very nasty shock because it dropped through the other hole. One brave male customer fished out her bag for her. Everybody except the poor lady concerned found it highly amusing.'

Mr J. R. Pawsey, Norwich: 'I grew up in the village of Alpheton, in west Suffolk, and throughout my childhood, right into my teens, I knew no other form of sanitation. The funniest story I can relate concerns a young man whose proud possession was a two-seater, open-topped car. In the late 1930s, he persuaded a young lady to go to the pictures with him at Sudbury. They spent a delightful evening at the cinema and on their way home to Long Melford, it became rather foggy. Car lights in those days were not very good and they collided with the rear of the night soil cart. This was full and the impact forced the contents first one way (over the horse) and then the other way covering the bonnet and windscreen of the two-seater car, sending 'deposits' into the laps of the young people.'

Mr Neave, Attleborough: 'For years, my father emptied our skip (a large, galvanised, wide bucket) on a midden (dung hill or rubbish heap) across the road where he had a horse and carriage hire business. It is interesting to relate that when he sold the business, the transfer of the deeds had a clause enabling father to use the midden for as long as he required it.'

Mr Roy Larkins, Lowestoft: 'There is a "bumby" standing in all its Victorian splendour in Belle Vue Park, Lowestoft, and I assume it has been there since the park opened on 28th March 1874. My family was offered the gatekeeper's cottage in the park in 1938. The "bumby" had a dual use. The door facing the cottage was for the family's use but the other side had a similar section for the use of the park's gardeners, of whom my father was one.'

Mr J. Main, Brandon: 'During the years 1930–38, our family lived in Feltwell. We shared one outside loo between two families. Normally, it worked quite well as the lady next door lived with just an aged father but when visitors called, mostly young people, we were often seen with our legs crossed, hanging around the door. As there was no able-bodied man next door, the task of emptying fell to my father. As a young lad, it was my job to hold the lantern – I often got it wrong by holding it in such a way that Dad was unable to see. My other job was to burn rags to offset the odour as Dad ladled the contents from

The brick-built privy in Belle Vue Park used by Roy Larkins and his family in the 1930s. (J. Arnold)

the pit to the hole in the garden. That job took about three hours. Mother would have a hot drink ready on our return. I remember the lady next door only smoked when attending the loo, the smoke would pour out of the wire-mesh, 1 ft window. On the night of the Joe Louis v Tommy Farr fight, a boar pig from a nearby farm ran loose in our garden. Dad and I went to drive it away when it suddenly charged out of the bushes. Dad shouted, "In the little house, quick." The boar butted the door many times before our dog drove it away. Dad later told me that had it broken down the door, he was prepared to put me down the large hole, out of harm's way – what a thought – saved from what?!'

Mrs Joyce Preston, Bungay: 'Dad always kept a good vegetable garden. Mum said that after the water was laid on the vegetables were never the same again! Our cat raised many litters in a large cardboard box complete with warm blankets in the outside loo. We also had a little evacuee for two or three years during the war and I don't think she could make out what on earth it was when she first saw that bucket!'

Mr E. Thorpe, Barking: 'The older folk always had a fetish about "inner cleanliness" – my grandparents would lace their tea with Epsom Salts on a regular basis; it was prudent to decline a cup of Granny's tea on that particular evening. The salts would upset even the most hardened of stomachs and induce a condition known as "the trots"'.

Mr D. R. Gates, Sudbourne: 'We lived in a small, isolated cottage where water came from a well and where there were bucket toilets, paraffin house lamps and wood burning stoves. We had an abundance of vegetables all year round. The garden was the reception area for "chucking the bucket"; the contents of which were an important part of crop manuring and rotation, so much so that the buckets would not be emptied just any-where but in a pre-planned order just as methodical as modern-day farming. All the "best" families had at least two buckets – a clean one for the changeover. My grandfather often told the fol-lowing story:

'The local barber in this small town would keep open very late on Saturdays in order that customers could get a shave after the pubs closed and attend church on Sundays without any stubble. Now the night soil cart had turned into the street oppo-site the barber's and was halfway up the hill when all hell was let loose. A fire had broken out and taken hold in some that-ched cottages. When the firemen got to the station, there was no horse to pull the fire engine. Realising the council had only one horse for the two operations, a fierce argument erupted as to

100

priority. In the end, the brigade came out on top and hastily removed Dobbin from the shafts of the night soil cart.

'Unfortunately, they had forgotten to check the wheels and the whole outfit went sailing down the hill and crashed into the barber's shop. A bulletin was displayed on the council notice-board next day:

"The Council wish to apologise for any inconvenience caused due to unforeseen circumstances when the night soil collection service had to be terminated at short notice. A temporary disposal pit has been created on waste land near the crossroads and will be open until midnight Mon-Sat. It is hoped to have the tank in operation shortly. In the meantime, a number of large wheelbarrows are available at the Council Depot for those who need bucket transport." '

Pam and Ron Rowe, Saxmundham: 'Childhood memories – every Sunday morning, the men could be seen walking to their allotments, with a funny shaped pail covered with a cloth, their pipes blowing clouds of smoke, as this was the day the "donigans" were emptied. In 1943, a lady in the village was reaching for a nice ripe plum and fell head first into a large prepared hole. Lucky for her, a neighbour saw her legs sticking in the air and pulled her out. Her first thought was for her false teeth – she pushed her arm into the mess and found them, held them under a water pump, gave them a clean and put them back in her mouth.'

Josephine Burrows, Stowmarket: 'I have agonising memories as a child, venturing down the garden with a hurricane lantern which always seemed to cast weird shadows on dark nights. My mother would stand at the door but would not come. She was very strict and hoped I would overcome my fears and learn to stand on my own two feet. But we were healthy, with good plain food, and many days spent outside. Can you imagine what the present generation would think?'

Alan J. Page, Stowmarket: 'In our village, the lower classes used to refer to the lavatory as the "shithouse", pronounced "shittuss", or "privy", whilst respectable spinster ladies referred to it as the "coffee shop". The upper classes referred to it as "the House of Commons". The larger houses had a pool bumby – a convenience with no pail but a deep pit, with sufficient capacity for six months. A friend of mine from Kenya tells me that such a convenience was known as "the long drop".'

Pat West, Leiston: 'We lived in Hacheston post office years ago. The cold tap was put in when I was three and a bathroom when I was just ten, in time for me to start grammar school. Mother was pleased because I could invite friends home as we now had a flush. All my friends who lived in council houses had outdoor flush loos – luxury! When the bathroom was built, Father moved the loo to an old stable and couldn't understand the foul smell in there. I never explained I was collecting mole skins in an old bird's nest, hidden in there amongst the newspaper collected for recycling for the church.'

Mr D. Kersey, Leiston: 'As a child, I lived near Aldeburgh, in Suffolk. In October of each year, Father would dig a huge hole; my brother and I would be prepared for the annual ritual of emptying. We were attired in old clothes, the girls were shut inside and neighbours warned. We all donned muslin masks and Father used a long-handled implement like a large soup spoon. It usually took about two hours. Mother would have hot water ready so we could bathe in the old tin bath in front of the kitchen fire. The old clothes were burnt.'

Mrs Kelly Shannon, Martlesham Heath: 'The local school had a row of such toilets and I have heard it said that the young lads used to gather a long bunch of stinging nettles and lift up the back of the teachers' loo, extending the nettles to catch their bottoms, then watch the unfortunate teachers scratching themselves which, of course, caused a real titter throughout the class. Mother used to hang bunches of lavender from two hooks under the inside of the lavatory window.'

Mrs Jean Jerman, Reydon: 'During the war years (1939–1945), we were always petrified that a bomb or a doodle-bug would drop on us. We all attended the Methodist Sunday school in the Methodist Chapel; their toilets were a classic. They were called "bumbies". One would sit on a wooden seat and whatever one "passed" went into a deep hole below. That was fine as long as there was an avalanche every now and then to make room for more. At the rear were little doors which the boys (including my brother) delighted in opening to have a peep at us girls relieving ourselves before or after Sunday school.'

B. T. Bone, Snape: 'In the early 1950s, my late grandmother, Kitty Crane, lived in a cottage in Snape. Her brick toilet was down the garden. One day I saw Gran making her way down; she was a large lady. I waited until she was inside, then gently removed the board at the back and tickled her bum with a nettle. She almost ran back to the house and told Mum there was a rat in the privy. "Of course there isn't", Mum said. "I know there is," Gran said, "it just bit my arse." '

Mrs O. Armstrong, Stowmarket: 'We used to have central heating in our outside loo! My husband fixed a pig light/heater which was switched on indoors so that by the time we had waded through deep snow, it was heaven to sit in the warm. We used to keep two or three pigs: one year they got swine fever so we dug a very deep hole to bury them. Instead of covering them up, we used the hole to empty the bucket and just scattered a little soil each time. For several weeks, my husband used to say, "I'm just going to bury the body." I wouldn't wish for that again but there were lots of lovely things that did happen in those days.'

John B. Catchpole, Lowestoft: 'My grandfather was the land-lord of a Suffolk fishing village pub. It had a row of outside toilets each with a collection tin. Each tin carried a full comple-ment at the end of the week. One night, Grandfather was woken by a commotion: apparently, one of the collector's techni-ques was to carry the full tin on his head and the bottom had literally collapsed around his ears.

'Also, our village was divided into two parts, with the church located on a fairly steep hill. During the Second World War, an armed soldier was posted at this lonely spot halfway down the hill; the night was foggy and the sentry did not hear the approaching night soil cart. He did, however, see a ghostly shape silently gliding down the hill. He raised his rifle to chal-lenge the "stranger" but terror took control of his trigger finger and he loosed off a round over the horse's head. The horse took off at a gallop down the hill. On a slight bend in the road stood my school. The playground formed an ideal escape route for the cart driver, who, while he managed to stop the cart, was unable to prevent it from "turning turtle". We did not miss school the next day but we were told to mind where we put our feet!'

John Linder, Banningham: 'One gentleman neighbour I lived near as a lad had a regular habit mid-morning each day: armed with his newspaper, he would proceed to his outdoor loo. One day, painters were giving the exteriors of the cottages a fresh coat of white Snowcem. Unnoticed, I borrowed a tin and a large brush, tiptoed to the rear of the loos, silently opened the rear of the gentleman's loo and vigorously gave his backside a good coat of Snowcem. I disappeared quickly – he jumped out of the loo with his trousers around his ankles. My mother and two other ladies were talking in the garden and he bellowed, "Which of you painted my a...?"

'On another occasion, two of the ladies were in their respective loos and were talking. I borrowed Mother's linen line, threaded it through the handles and tied them tightly together. They were inside for two hours before being discovered.'

Mrs Peggy Knock, Mendlesham, Suffolk: 'In the 1930s, whilst visiting my grandmother in Ipswich, I was stopped from using the outside privy because "Mrs B. from next door was down there". Granny shared the same loo – anyway, I had to wait until Mrs B. came back (watching from behind the kitchen net curtains) before I could venture forth. Perhaps this was the forerunner of Neighbourhood Watch!'

Harold I. Reeder remembers converting an old farmhouse into a modern dwelling in the 1960s: 'When it was completed, the lady of the house threw a children's party and was very concerned about the very frequent visits to the toilet by the children, generally in groups. It became evident later that hers was the only "flush" in the village.'

A quite-the-opposite story from Mrs Horne of Leiston: 'The height of my happy memories was the "Bumby" out in Grandad's shed. To we townies this was a wonderful treat. How innocent can you be as a child?'

In her book *Life Behind the Cottage Door*, Valerie Porter writes about a new council tenant's mahogany WC seat being removed to make a fine frame for 'Grandad's photograph', and an old villager on being asked if she liked her new indoor plumbed bath, replied with feeling, 'Thank God, Sir, I has never had occasion to use it!'

Another true tale – In the 1960s, one old villager who lived by himself had a flush toilet installed indoors. He certainly found the indoor convenience to his liking, since outside trips were getting to be uncomfortable because of his gout. The trouble was that nobody had explained its workings and so he used it as and when, in an excited sort of way. Unrestrained, he didn't think to pull the chain after use. Indeed, a few days passed before an unfortunate relative called and found the insalubrious mess. The education of the user was of the utmost priority.

Finally, Mrs P. Banham of Pakefield recalls: 'I was born in Beach Street, Pakefield, earlier this century. We were the last to live in these cottages before the sea engulfed them in the 1930s. I well remember how frightening it was when there were heavy gales and high tides because the sea came right up to our back garden. Our outside toilet was at the very bottom of the garden – one night walking back to the house after using this loo, Father heard a noise and, as he turned, he saw the loo disappear down the cliff. He often laughed and said if he had stopped and fastened his leather belt he would have gone down with it.'

[11]

CHAMBER POTS

The sun may shine, the wind may blow,
It may be light, it may well be dark.
But when you've gotta go, you've gotta go,
Never mind that the dog may bark.

Trotting outside last thing at night to empty the bladder or
appease the bowel was all very well but what was a person
expected to do if the stomach turned somersaults in the very
middle of the night?

Well, a modicum of comfort was secured for watery waste.
The chamber pot was a convenient container with a handle,
which sat under every bed, but it only scored as a convenience
if a person wanted to do a 'number one'. Anything extra which
required shifting meant a rush outside into the cold night air.

A demand for skill and judgment was essential when using
this vessel, often referred to by country people as the 'piss pot'.
As it only reached a few inches above the ground, responsible
users squatted low. Larger folk no doubt found this toiletry task
quite difficult; piddling from an awkward height into such a
small receptacle was fraught with problems, and targeting one's
water was essential.

Although the indoor chamber pot cannot by any stretch of
the imagination be viewed as a lavish alternative, it beat rushing
outside in the dead of night. For women, particularly, it was an
attractive convenience since they possess not men's assemblage –
the male species can hang out of a window quite easily (sorry
about the sash window mate – how was I to know it had a
weakness and would come crashing down at a crucial moment!).

King's Lynn museum has a wonderful collection of chamber pots. (J. Arnold)

Lucky households boasted one chamber pot per bedroom. Communal ones were rough on the family, and constant vigilance was necessary to ascertain their capacity – 'I have every reason to believe there is room for one more piddle in there.' Spillages were unhygienic and much frowned upon by the lady of the house.

The average-sized chamber pot accepted around five pints of fluid. Many will be vague about the amounts of human water wastage during the night. Having put this to the test, I can assure you that a five pint pot services around five adults. On average, a pint a piddle. Of course, this does not take into account members of the household who have been out on the beer all evening, and who could most probably fill a whole chamber pot by themselves.

Not an attractive statistic but nevertheless one that could be well worth knowing.

When we were young, Mother took advantage of a large hallway and placed two chamber pots there. Unfortunately, it was also home to a wardrobe with a mirror. Mother had been warmly tucked up in bed one evening when nature called. Her teeth out and hair in curlers, she stumbled her way into the hall and plonked herself on the chamber pot, facing the mirror. Father heard a pathetic shout of fright. Upon enquiry, he discovered Mother, in her half-asleep state, had spied herself in the wardrobe mirror, and instantly thought we had burglars!

Bobby Benton's *The Honeycart Song* contains the immortal words:
  'They wunt orol on this lektrick owt in the sticks yew know
  An I recorl a'cowld dark nite I saw this torch aglow.
  As I wuz gorn up ter fetchit he wuz cummin down.
  As we parst he say "Wotcher mearte", I say "Gernite Mr
    Brown".
  Cors owt thar in the country them howses arnt harf spred
    abowt.
  An sunhow I dunt know how I missed this woman owt,
  Nex' tyme I went rownd theer she corld me a silly ole fewle.
  I dint care, I say, "Look heer, yew shodder dugger hole."
  But I tryed ter pleaze mer customers, the yung as well's th'
    owld.
  But they woont go owt in the deddar nite ter sit theer in th'
    cowld.
  Country fook arnt sorft yer know, they hev a rasarve insted,

An, thass innits plarce fer an emarjency, an' they keep it
unner the bed!'

Let us consider then the disadvantages of night. Sandwiched
between warm comfortable sheets, it was almost an offence if
nature called for a 'number two'. Once your mind was made
up, it was necessary to rouse yourself from a delicious sleep and
set about attiring yourself in suitable clothing for that trip down
the garden path. Whether it was summer or winter, leaving a
warm 'pit' was an occasion that demanded something more than
a nightdress or a pair of pyjamas, as even a hot summer's night
could be comparatively cold after a warm bed. Country women
were positive thinkers and tried their best in the comfort stakes.
Hats, coats and Wellington boots were always placed appro-
priately by the back door. Torches too were placed in accessible
places. The wise housewife would often keep a spare torch or
candle and matches inside the outside loo, leaving little to
chance.

Needless to say, the casting shadows of night played tricks on
tired brains. Children, particularly, found the night-time excur-
sions very frightening and would rouse a parent to accompany
them down the eerie garden path. Relieved, further relief came
in the return of sweet and easy sleep. Insomniacs really ought to
try this trip. It's a wild kind of place outside at night and really
gets the heartbeat going.

Moonlit nights were shrouded in mystery and so the call of
nature was not always uninteresting, and the peace and quiet
could be a joy. My father was a herdsman all his life and up at
the crack of dawn. He always reckoned the rest of us were
missing the best part of the day. However, cold, wet and wintry
nights were a menace, and there were few compensations.

A fart it is a useful thing, it gives a body ease
It warms the bed in wintertime and drives away the fleas.

I have a couple of chamber pots which I use as plant holders. They add a lot of interest to a home and are always a talking point. Even the very shy laugh at the ribald comments. If you happen to have a Wemyss ware pot with unusual decoration, or a 17th–18th century stoneware pot with applied decoration, take it to Christie's, the Fine Art Auctioneers. To date they have not come across either of these but each would make an individual

The author's collection of chamber pots – now providing a marvellous decorative feature for the home. (Truth is, I can't bear to part with them!)

lot at auction.

In his *Direction to Servants* manual of 1745, Jonathan Swift found the whole idea of chamber pots distasteful. He wrote for the housemaid:

'I am very much offended with those Ladies, who are so proud and lazy, that they will not be at pains of stepping into the garden to pluck a rose (use the outside privy) but keep an odious implement, sometimes in the bedchamber itself, or at least in a dark closet adjoining, which they make use of to ease their worse necessities; and you are the usual carriers away of the pan, which maketh not only the chamber, but even their clothes offensive, to all who come near. Now, to cure them of the odious practice, let me advise you, on whom this office lieth, to convey away this utensil, that you will do it openly, down the great stairs, and in the presence of the footmen: and, if anybody knocketh, to open the street door, while you have the vessel in your hands: this, if anything can, will make your lady take the pains of evacuating her person in the proper place, rather than expose her filthiness to all the men servants in the house.'

This was an upper crust view. Poorer country people, however, sought consolation in a mutual commiseration. Their houses were much smaller and so they did everything together and witnessed each other's shortcomings in any case; piddling in front of one another was the least of their worries. Besides, the working classes had to empty the vessels themselves. If they were not worried, why bother about anyone else!

Although the chamber pot was intended for biological needs, the contents were beneficial for chilblains. Properties in the piddle were potently good for this nasty complaint. I can vouch for this, having suffered the most atrocious chilblains as a teenager.

My heels in winter often cracked, making walking very painful. Time and again, my dear mother advised me to sink my feet into a full chamber pot. Time and again, I refused point blank – until one day my feet were causing me such misery I just had to give Mum's idea a try. Flinching, I dipped my extremities, itching like mad after being in a warm bed and paining me stupid, into the night's collection of human watery waste. I allowed the warmish water to flow around my feet. Relief of some sort was almost immediate and I began a remarkable acceptance. If Mum's theory worked, I would at least be able to put on my new shoes and walk in a semblance of comfort.

Sitting about with smelly feet was a bit of a mistake in that our pet dog found me attractive company, but, after the process had been repeated a couple more times during the day, my distress eased. Soon I could get my shoes on. That was over 30 years ago and, touch wood, (done) to this day I have never been bothered with chilblains. The cure must surely be attributed to the contents of the chamber pot.

[12]

SCHOOLS AND PUBLIC PLACES

I attended Stoke Holy Cross Primary School, near Norwich, and I vividly remember the block of outside loos which were emptied each week into the school garden. The girls' toilet block (and presumably the boys' one around the other side) were separated into about four cubicles. However, the waste all found its way to a common concrete pit below. And didn't it seem a long way down. I feared for my safety at a very early age.

I was well used to the outside earth closet and had great faith in my father's management of the same. But with the school pit you could actually hear your deposits drop, and the water, once untapped, seemed to take forever before it splashed far down below. I felt very sorry for the nice caretaker man who had the unpleasant task of raking it all out once a week.

The toilet block was situated quite a few yards from the school cloakroom back door, but we had quick access to coats should the weather be raw or wet. Play times saw a mad dash outside, and it was a wonder no one got hurt. But it did not matter because we were all young, energetic, and strong in mind – a little thing like an outside privy was not going to hamper our play. Most country schools used this same method; it was all perfectly normal, and by the time I left at the age of eleven, my fears had long fled.

Modern schoolchildren have been modernised to flushing away their cares but may still have to brave all weathers by going outside to the toilet block. In fact, many teachers, and I wholeheartedly agree, see no good reason why it's necessary to move them inside. Children are cushioned enough from the harming aspects of society, a trip outdoors to the loo gives them

Marsham County Primary School was built in 1852 and bumped along with the earliest pit method until modernised to flush. The little boys in the photograph seem quite unconcerned and will at least have wonderful stories to tell when they grow up.

a fresh air breathing space from lessons and blows away the cobwebs from tired, centrally-heated brains. Why, some would call the trip 'character building'!

Perhaps I have lived in the countryside too long but I am sure the outside situation does no harm – children are more resilient than we give them credit for. The only fears could be, these days, in the areas of safety and security. Norfolk County Council has had a 'blitz' on school toilets in the last few years, but not all councillors are convinced that the expense of providing inside facilities is justified. 'We've made good progress,' said one, 'but it's very important indeed that we make sure we don't waste money.'

A recent report reveals that many of the county's schools are reconciled to the situation. Some are quite unconcerned, although parent-teacher associations would generally like to be rid of outside toilets. In a lot of instances, however, there are no obvious places to site them inside. Some schools are listed buildings and so any great change is restricted. The Government may appear to lack sympathy, but then there must be more pressing problems to solve. It takes a lot to kill the enthusiasm of country children – I hardly think they are going to get depressed about not having indoor toilets.

One gentleman sent me a Norfolk Education Committee specification used earlier this century, *Standard Details of Purpose-Made Latrine Seat, with cover flap and bucket shield.* The hole size for infants was 8 inches × 5 inches, and for juniors and seniors 11 inches × 9 inches. The overall width was 20 inches, and the height for infants 10 inches, and for juniors and seniors 13½ inches.

Mr S. Gilbert from north Lowestoft has recollections of a village pub in the 1930s. 'When I reached the age of nine,' he remembers, 'I used to help on the farm which was part of the property belonging to the Wheel of Fortune public house, at Alpington. I helped the labourer to empty the toilets. As the person sat down, any liquid drained away and the solids dropped onto a concrete base below. I was responsible for spreading lime on top of the solids (usually Friday nights). When there was a good pile (usually during school holidays), I took a wheelbarrow and pushed it across the road to an adjoining field where I buried the solids in a farm manure heap. I then scrubbed out the whole emptying area and spread lime on the floor and base. I later spread the manure heap on the land which was then ploughed in.

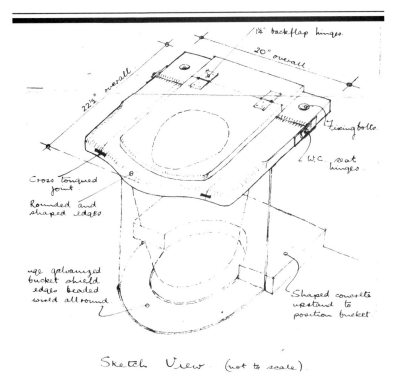

Sketch View (not to scale)

One gentleman sent me a Norfolk Education Committee specification used earlier this century, *Standard Details of Purpose-Made Latrine Seat, with cover flap and bucket shield*. The hole size for infants was 8 inches × 5 inches, and for juniors and seniors 11 inches × 9 inches. The overall width was 20 inches, and the height for infants 10 inches, and for juniors and seniors 13½ inches.

'Later on, lavatory pails were introduced; then I had to empty as often as was necessary but still on the manure heap or else I dug a hole in the field and buried it. I have related this story to various people who insist such places never existed in my lifetime.'

Author's note: There are many much younger than you who remember, Mr Gilbert. This book should convince them.

The substantial building at Felbrigg Hall, formerly an 18th century privy and now a summerhouse.

Felbrigg Hall in Norfolk is open to the public and possesses a spiffing old garden lavatory. It is a better example than I could ever have imagined – more like a miniature palace than a little back shed! Undeniably, there it stands behind the mansion, bold as brass, built of flint, brick and York stone. Very grand too it must have been when fully operational as an outside privy. It was constructed in 1752, to the order of its then owner, William Windham, who was a man of considerable thrift and ingenuity. The interior walls were glazed-tiled later – a late-Victorian after-thought – but the floor has always been made of the splendidly

118

simple 12 inches × 12 inches Norfolk brick pamments. The edifice extends to some 7 ft × 7 ft, and the back wall supported the seating arrangement. A letter from the then squire to his steward, written from London on 20th January 1752, says:

'I am very glad you have fixed a little house near the Bleach, the line drying area behind the mansion's laundry. I think it is the best place imaginable. Should not the inside be stuccoed and how many holes? There must be one for a child and I would have it as light as possible. There must be a good broad place to set a candle on and a place to keep paper. I think the holes should be wide and rather oblong and the seats broad and not quite level; rather low before but rising behind. Though the plainer the better it should be neat.'

This 'little house' was converted to a summerhouse over 20 years ago, minor repairs and re-roofing revealing some fascinating details of construction, long since forgotten. The necessary pit beneath the 'seats' extended for some 18 inches outside the building, and the 24 inch rear wall was supported on three well constructed brick arches. Towards the top of the pit was a beautifully built 12 inches × 12 inches brick drainage tunnel sloping down under the old laundry and dairy, picking up their drainage too and then connecting into the main 2 ft 6 inches × 2 ft brick canal which carried all the discharge from the mansion to be disposed of in the park.

[13]

EMBARRASSING MOMENTS
IN PUBLIC PLACES

'A man with a mission', old Bert smiled a toothless grin as yet
another cricketer ran with a certain amount of urgency behind
the cricket pavilion. Ah, yes! The gentle thud of willow upon
leather – it wasn't all cricket. There can't be many sports-loving
people who haven't had to content themselves with less than
favourable lavatory conditions. The sight of the little wooden
structure was often an added cause for merriment – 'You mean
to say you invited us down here for this?'

Country clubhouses were generally wooden, painted white
and sporting not much more than a pretty verandah. Generous
ladies spent the afternoon kissing young children, and preparing
cucumber sandwiches for tea. The whole outing was a fun time
for many families in the soaring heat of a Sunday afternoon, but
younger female spectators often dreaded the point at which they

would have to make a visit in full view of the field and other spectators; it was not good manners to enquire about their health when they left their seat! Trouble was, cricket matches usually took place when the flies were most rampant. Peering through half-closed lids due to the brilliant sun, you entered the small hut to find that some person who had gone before had forgotten to close the back socket – in other words, the lid was not where it should have been. A flair with a fly-swat was a must if you wanted to rid the underneath of buzzing flies. Black-mailing insects are no picnic.

Have you ever jived to Bill Haley, or jittered to the sound of Glenn Miller in a village hall? Then, the chances are you probably did a lot of your socialising in rather romantic-looking, wooden-type buildings, eying up the local talent. The consequences of too much drinking meant plenty of piddling in outside toilets which were not exactly stylish affairs. They were practical places for down to earth country people – comfort was the last thing a person could expect. 'Cor blimey, I saw this great, dirty, black mass laying in the darkness. It grunted and I turned it over. It were old Charlie spewing his 'ead off in the bog.'

Freshly cleaned toilet pails awaited business every Saturday night. They were usually in unlit, dark and cold places which were not entirely designed to linger in for long, unless, of course, some chirpy and inebriated person happened to be pranking about outside. Certainly you did not need to be a detective to find the convenience – their constant usage meant the solitary pail filled up quickly.

Of course, these privies were often some distance from the village hall. No matter that the sky was blazing with a fairyland of stars – if it happened to be frosty outside, it was darned uncomfortable having to wait, perhaps in an off-the-shoulder,

121

special frock, for an indefinite time until some other person vacated the seat.

Young men being what they are when full of drink would often play a trick on some of the unfortunate young ladies who were occupying the outside convenience. Armed with a healthy bunch of nettles they had secured from a nearby verge, they would unlatch the rear disposal door and in quite an unsophisticated way would tickle the bare bums whilst, perhaps, whistling softly. They left the unamused young ladies seething in agony. Unfeeling, they found it a huge joke. I am sure many is the time a young country lad has been slapped across the face with a young country girl's handbag after such an incident. 'You wait, Jimmy Cross, I'm going to get my big brother onto you.'

Today's population is on the move. Caravanning is popular and enthusiasts are well used to the chemical toilet. They do not regard it as a hindrance but a super convenience – it beats bopping behind a bush thick with stinging nettles! Gone are the days when outdoor camping meant exercising discretion. Helen, a lovely lady, well into her eighties, recalls her Girl Guide days:

'Once a location had been chosen, two adults went before and dug a long trench in a secluded corner of a field. Two boards were put across this trench onto which an old tea-chest was placed; two holes already having been cut out, one at the top to a suitable girth for the girls' bottoms, and another larger hole at the bottom for the waste to drop through into the dug pit below. The whole was shrouded in canvas and a fir cone tied onto a piece of string, strategically placed when in residence, to advertise it being in use. At the end of the week, the trench was filled in and the turf which had been watered all week, was laid back – as if nobody had been!'

No chemicals here – but the makeshift privy had to be emptied at the end of the Higham point-to-point meeting.

Of course, we have entered the hi-tech '90s, but there are still many country pursuits, events and shows where the toileting arrangements have little sympathy for the faint-hearted. All part and parcel of a fresh-air-filled day out in the country. This photograph was taken a couple of years ago at a Suffolk point-to-point event; rather like the Girl Guides that Helen recalls, in that these portable loos were encased in a huge tent and partitioned off separately. Canvas flaps were the only divide between the queue and the person in residence. There was little finesse and a lot of guesswork. In fact, no room for error at all, 'I am dreadfully sorry; I thought this one was empty'...

FOOTNOTE

Young people reading this book will most probably find it hard to believe that we performed our toilet in this relaxed manner. I reiterate, there was no other way – we knew nothing else. Certainly we do not wish them to feel sorry for us, in fact, I consider us quite fortunate in that we had a chance to be so self-sufficient.

I sometimes wonder if those who commend today's sanitary arrangements and condemn those of years gone by realise what happens when they 'take the train' – that what they do in the neat little lavatory compartments actually falls out onto the track as the Inter-City speeds its way across the countryside. That is why passengers are requested 'NOT TO GO WHEN THE TRAIN IS IN THE STATION'...

Suffice to say, all those who used the outside privy had a wonderfully flexible attitude to life and enjoyed laughing at anything that moved or stank!

It may be just another statistic but did you know that Britain alone pumps over 300 million gallons of sewage into the sea around our coasts every single day? Hardly surprising that people now think twice before taking a dip. Another natural joy denied us because of the modern flush! And at what cost do we flush! Water companies spend millions on purifying water for us to use and much of that beautifully clean water goes into flushing the indoor toilet. If that is not a criminal waste, then I am indeed more ignorant that I thought I was. But wait, some people of common-sense are questioning this so-called step into progress. With recycling now firmly implanted in politicians' minds, interest is growing in finding ways of turning the contents of the toilet into a productive, economic, environmentally friendly and safe compost. Since the introduction of septic tanks (which are found in almost 50% of villages) and mains sewage, the use of human waste in the garden has been forgotten and the soil is objecting to this lack of conditioner.

Adam West of Wenhaston, in Suffolk, is doing something about it. He is developing domestic ideas based on Scandinavian produced 'biological' toilets, which he imports. These can be installed in outhouses and sheds for practical garden use; more sophisticated versions are available for the home. His system uses no chemicals and works by anaerobic means, producing compost with the help of air and warmth, and additions of materials such as sawdust and wood chippings.

Two of these have been installed – one at Hinton and one at Walpole – and Adam is monitoring their performance. He has a lifelong interest in the environment and has attended a course on human-waste composting at the Centre for Alternative Technology in Wales, and, along with increasing numbers of others, feels there is no reason why we shouldn't enjoy our flush conditions but use the waste to enrich our gardens. I, for one, think this is the only way forward.

AND FINALLY...

Laughs are short on the ground these days – jokes were part of everyday life with the outside privy. 'Crikey, I never thought I'd seen mountains till I looked in the pail. Dad's was the highest of them all, which reminds me, Dad, when are you going to empty it?'

Apart from splashing one's backside in the modern flush, nothing out of the ordinary happens any more. It's all so unexcitingly predictable and uneventful!

A PRIVY BY ANY OTHER NAME

A 'certain' place
Asterroom
Biffy
Bog
Boghouse
Bombay
Chamber of commerce
Chamberlain pianos ('bucket
  lav')
Chuggie
Closet
Comfort station
Crapphouse
Crapping castle
Crapping kennel
Dike
Dinkum-dunnies
Dunnekin
Dunnick
Dyke
Doneks
Dubs
Duffs
Dunnekin
Garden loo
Garder robe
Gong house
Gong
Go and have a Jimmy Riddle
Go and have a Tim Tit

Going to pick daisies
Going to see a man about a
  dog
Going to stack the tools
Going to the George
Going to the groves
Gone where the wind is
  always blowing
Heads
Here is are
Holy of holies
Honk
House of commons
House of office
Houses of parliament
Jakes
Jerry-come tumble
Jericho
Karzi
Klondike
Larties
Latrine
Lavatory
Little house
My aunts
Nessy
Netty
Out the back
Petty
Place of easement

Place of repose
Place of retirement
Reading room
Round-the-back
Shit-hole
Shittush
Shooting gallery
Shunkie
Slash house
The backhouse
The boggy at the Bottom
The bush
The dispensary
The dunny
The grot
The halting station Hoojy-boo
(attributed to Dame Edith
Evans)
The house where the emperor
goes on foot
The hum
The jakers
The jampot
The japping
The John
The lats
The long drop
The opportunity
The ping-pong house
The proverbial
The Sammy
The shants
The shot-tower

The sociable
The tandem (a two-holer)
The thinking house
The throne room
The watteries
The wee house
The whajucallit
Three and more seaters
Thunder box
Two seaters
Widdlehouse
Windsor Castle
'Yer Tiz'

Especially for WCs:
Adam & Eve
Chain of events
Flushes and blushes
The penny house
The plumbing
The porcelain pony
The water box
Umtag (Russian version of the
WC)
Going to inspect the plumbing
The urinal
Waterloo

The term 'privy' is an Early
Middle English word which
derives from the Latin 'pri-
vatus' meaning apart or
secret.